A Magick as Old as the Hills

The anglo-Celtic religions are the most popular traditions among today's magickal community. Those who look exclusively to British and Irish sources to revive that tradition overlook the rich folk magick of southern Appalachia, where many Scottish and English immigrants settled as long ago as the mid-1700s.

Because the Appalachian folk lived in virtual isolation from the rest of the country for many decades, their old magickal beliefs remained largely intact until the intrusion of more modern beliefs during this century. Even though these people lived in an area where a secure home or even a pair of shoes were considered luxury items, their magickal spells focus on improving the overall harmony of their lives, rather than financial well-being. Their brand of folk magick thus focuses on omens, portents, curses, cures, and protections. These spells—which facilitate healing, fertility, household tasks, hunting and fishing, love, childbirth, favorable weather, protection from mishaps, and more—will add a rich new dimension to your magickal practice, whatever your tradition.

Instead of treating Appalachian folk magick as a quaint superstition, Edain McCoy presents a legitimate magickal system that you can use to make a difference in your life. (This book also can be comfortably used by those with spiritual traditions not generally considered "magickal," such as Christianity.) Learn how to harmoniously integrate these spells and rituals into your current practices, and discover how this dying art can expand your magickal horizons.

About the Author

Edain McCoy became a self-initiated Witch in 1981, and has been an active member of the Pagan community since her 1983 formal initiation into a large San Antonio coven. She has been researching alternative and Pagan spiritualities since her teens, when she was first introduced to Kaballah (Jewish mysticism). Today she is a part of the Wittan Irish Pagan Tradition and a Priestess of Brighid in that tradition. An alumnus of the University of Texas (BA in history), she currently pursues part-time graduate and undergraduate studies at Indiana University. Edain has taught classes in guided meditation and automatic writing, and occasionally works with students who wish to study Wiccan and Celtic Witchcraft. A native Hoosier, she is a member of The Indiana Historical Society, The Authors Guild, The Wiccan/Pagan Press Alliance, and is a former woodwind player for the Lynchburg (VA) Symphony. A descendant of the infamous feuding McCoy family of Kentucky, Edain also proudly claims as a forefather Sir Roger Williams, the seventeenth-century religious dissenter.

To Write to the Author

If you wish to contact the author or would like more information about this book, please write to the author in care of Llewellyn Worldwide, and we will forward your request. Both the author and publisher appreciate hearing from you and learning of your enjoyment of this book and how it has helped you. Llewellyn Worldwide cannot guarantee that every letter written to the author can be answered, but all will be forwarded. Please write to:

Llewellyn's New Worlds of Mind and Spirit
P.O. Box 64383, Dept. K671-8, St. Paul, MN 55164-0383, U.S.A.
Please enclose a self-addressed, stamped envelope for reply, or $1.00 to cover costs.
If outside the U.S.A., enclose international postal reply coupon.

Llewellyn's Practical Magick Series

Mountain Magick

(previously titled: *In a Graveyard at Midnight*)

Folk Wisdom From the Heart of Appalachia

Edain McCoy

1997
Llewellyn Publications
St. Paul, Minnesota, 55164-0383, U.S.A.

Mountain Magick. Copyright © 1997 by Edain McCoy. All rights reserved. Printed in the United States of America. No part of this book may be used or reproduced in any manner whatsoever without written permission from Llewellyn Publications, except in the case of brief quotations embodied in critical articles or reviews.

FIRST EDITION
First Printing, 1997
(previously titled: *In a Graveyard at Midnight*)

Cover Art by Anthony Meadows
Cover Design by Anne Marie Garrison
Interior Art by Anthony Meadows, and Tom Grewe
Interior Design and Editing by Connie Hill

Neither author nor publisher in any way advocates the use of toxic herbs and other potentially harmful substances for either magick or medicine, and neither the author nor publisher can assume any responsibility for the side effects of experimentation with them.

Library of Congress Cataloging-in-Publication Data
McCoy, Edain, 1957-
   [In a graveyard at midnight]
   Mountain Magick : folk wisdom from the heart of Appalachia / Edain McCoy. — 1st ed.
        p.   cm. — (Llewellyn's practical magick series:)
   Includes bibliographical references and index.
   ISBN 1-56718-671-8
   1. Folklore—Appalachian Region, Southern. 2. Magic—Appalachian Region, Southern. 3. Traditional medicine—Appalachian Region, Southern. I. Title. II. Series.
GR108.M33   1997
398'.09756'8—dc21   97-17470
                                                                                                                CIP

Llewellyn Worldwide does not participate in, endorse, or have any authority or responsibility concerning private business transactions between our authors and the public.
    All mail addressed to the author is forwarded but the publisher cannot, unless specifically instructed by the author, give out an address or phone number.

Llewellyn Publications
A Division of Llewellyn Worldwide, Ltd.
St. Paul, Minnesota 55164-0383, U.S.A.

Llewellyn's Practical Magick Series

To some people, the idea that "Magick" is practical comes as a surprise. It shouldn't. The entire basis for Magick is to exercise influence over one's environment. Magick is an interactive process of spiritual growth and psychological transformation. Even so, the spiritual life rests firmly on material foundations. Magick is a way of life and must be lived, not just talked about, and that includes experiencing the wonders, pleasures and pains of material existence.

The material world and the spiritual are intertwined and it is this very interconnectedness that provides the Magickal Link, the magickal means for the spirit to influence the material, and vice versa.

Magick can be used in one's daily life for better living and in opening the doors to new worlds of mind and spirit. Each of us has been given Mind and Body, and it is our spiritual opportunity to make full use of these wonderful gifts. Mind and Body work together, and Magick is simply the extension of this interaction into dimensions beyond the limits normally perceived. That's why we commonly talk of the "supernormal" in connection with the domain of Magick.

The Body is alive, and all Life is an expression of the Divine. There is spiritual, Magickal power in the Body and in the Earth, just as there is in Mind and spirit. With Love and Will, we use Mind to link these aspects of Divinity together to bring about change. We add to the beauty of it all—for to work Magick we must work in concert with the Laws of Nature and of the Psyche. Magick is the flowering of our Human Potential.

Practical Magick is concerned with the Craft of living well, in harmony with the cycles of Nature and the seasons of the Earth. We increase the flow of Divinity in our lives, and in the world around us, through the things we make with hand and mind. All our acts of Will and desire are magickal acts.

Other Books by the Author

Witta: An Irish Pagan Tradition

A Witch's Guide to Faery Folk: Reclaiming Our Working Relationships With Invisible Helpers

How To Do Automatic Writing

The Sabbats: A New Approach to Living the Old Ways

Celtic Myth and Magick: Harness the Power of the Gods & Goddesses

The Sabbats: A New Approach to Living the Old Ways

Lady of the Night: A Handbook of Moon Magick and Ritual

Entering the Summerland: Customs and Rituals of Transition into the Afterlife

Inside a Witches' Coven

Forthcoming

Making Magick

Celtic Women's Mysteries

Thank you, thank you, thank you ....

When I first became interested in doing a book about the folk magick of Appalachia, I assumed that uncovering the needed information would be a relatively easy task. After all, I reasoned, if I could delve into the magick of the Celtic people whose civilization flourished in Europe some nine hundred years past, then certainly collecting magickal information from my own country and my own century should be a snap. Right?

Wrong.

I soon found out that the Appalachian magickal practices I sought, or—more importantly—would like to confirm, were often buried in hard-to-locate collections and books.

I want to thank all the wonderful folk in the libraries at Indiana University in Bloomington, and at the University of Kentucky in Lexington, for taking time to point me in the right direction whenever I got lost.

Also, a big thank you to the faculty and student assistants at the Folklore Institute at Indiana University for their helpful tips.

And a belated, but deeply felt, thank you to my elder McCoy relatives, now passed over, who first shared with me the magickal lore of the Appalachian Mountains.

A Word about the Language of this Book

While writing in non-sexist language is usually my preference, I found many cases in this book where the use of "he or she" or "him or her" to be just too cumbersome, and, in these instances, elected instead to use the masculine pronoun as a universal term indicating either gender.

Most of the expository material and magickal instructions are written in the present tense, even when the specific magickal practice under discussion is so old as to have become largely forgotten in Appalachia. This is so that the text will read smoothly and the reader will not have to endure jarring jumps in tense patterns.

The folkways are presented largely from the point of view of the mountain people so that, for example, when a sentence says "and after doing this you will never be sick again," it is making no promise of magickal success, but merely repeating what the Appalachian folk believe—or else believed in the not-too-distant past—to be true.

Followers of nature religions who refer to themselves as Witches will find that this term applies to a completely different sort of person in the mountains. Though it may be an inaccurate label, it is one which must be used in this text when referring to the magickal practitioners of the region since—like it or not—this is the word they use. The Appalachian point of view is detailed in Chapter One, along with an explanation of my system for differentiating between the two groups.

Contents

Introduction: Appalachia—A Twentieth Century Anomaly   xi

1 Folk Magick and the Mountains   1
    Folk Magick in Appalachia
    About Appalachian "Witches"
    Making Appalachian Folk Magick Work for You

2 Death, Dying, and "Haints"   19
    Of Lyches and the Graveyard
    Magical Self-Protection

3 The Magick of Health and Healing   41
    Tonics and Preventive Medicine and Magick

4 Weather Witching   73
    Mountain Beliefs about Meteorological Phenomena
    Making Weather Happen

5 Of Home, Hearth, and Earth   91
    The Magickal Mountain Home
    Gardening and Farming "By the Signs"
    Omens From the Land and Its People
    Omens and Magick of Animals

6 Love, Marriage, and Fidelity   125
    Old Maids and Love Divinations
    Mountain Spells for Love and Romance
    Magick and the Mountain Marriage

7 Fertility, Childbirth, and Children 147
    Fertility Magick and Divination
    Pregnancy Taboos and Safeguards
    Magick and Omens for and about Babies and Children

8 Integrating Appalachian Folk Magick with Your Own Magickal Lifestyle 169
    Choosing Appalachian Folk Spells for Your Own Use
    One Last Word on Graveyard Magick

Appendix A: Resources for Making Mountain Magick 181

Appendix B: Traditional Recipes of Southern Appalachia 187

Appendix C: Glossary of Terms 191

Bibliography and Source Materials (Partially Annotated) 199

Index 205

INTRODUCTION

Appalachia—A Twentieth Century Anomaly

I'm just a poor wayfaring stranger,
Traveling through this world of woe,
But there's no toll or sweat or danger,
In the world to which I go.
I'm going home to see my loved ones,
I'm going home no more to roam.
I'm just a poor wayfaring stranger
A long way from home.
　　　　　　　—Traditional Mountain Air

For over 2,400 miles, from Quebec to Alabama, the Appalachian Mountains rise from the Piedmont Plateau like a great blue barrier, as if their sentient purpose might have once been to keep the curious locked on the Atlantic seaboard, their eyes never to behold the vast wonders of the North American continent which lay beyond. Geologically, this mountain range is much older than her steeper, more rugged cousins to the west. Rocks dating from the Precambrian era (beginning no earlier than 700,000,000 years ago) have been found on her slopes, so old they contain no traces of fossilized plant life.[1]

Time has softened the Appalachian range, gentled her rocky face; her many seasons have sculpted her soft curves and molded her deep, windy valleys. In the steepest and most impenetrable region of this range, the southern heart of Appalachia, permanent civilization came relatively late. The Native American tribespeople we know today as the Cherokee were among the first settlers of the southern mountains. Archaeological evidence dates their occupation of the mountains to at least 500 C.E.[2] They called the southern Appalachians "the blue hills of God."[3] In the Cherokee creation myth, it was a giant bird descending from heaven whose beating wings dried the muddy, primordial sea. Having done so, the bird then fell down upon the earth to die of exhaustion, her crumpled body leaving its own memorial as it formed the steep ridges and hills of Appalachia. Taking pity upon her, heaven covered her body with trees and flowers and running streams, then invited her children to come live there so that the bird should never be lonely, nor her efforts forgotten.

Over a thousand years later came the Europeans, first the Spanish explorers in 1540, then, two centuries later, the English and Scots. Many of the latter brought with them rigid Calvinistic beliefs which decreed that the mountains (along with the rest of the earth) were created by no less than the hand of God, in 4004 B.C.E., and not a moment sooner.[4] Last came the geologists, whose explanation of the origin of the mountain range goes back millions of years, to when the primordial land mass, Pangaea, first began to separate into continents.

Throughout American history there has been a need to understand just how these awe-inspiring mountains, which stretch so far and wide, came to be. Perhaps convincing ourselves that we know when and how they were born makes them more manageable, less intimidating to those of us who do not live with their rhythms and cycles on a daily basis. Those who have made this beautiful, but harsh, range their home seek only to live with the land and its nature, and do not struggle against it as those of us outside the region are often compelled to do. Perhaps this is why mountain-dwellers have been content to allow time to pass more slowly, to take change in small doses, and to look with suspicion on "outlanders" who come into the hills seeking to impose on them their unfamiliar ways. And perhaps this is why so many old ways still persist in the remote hills.

Though I have never lived in the Appalachian Mountains (pronounced, as the natives will tell you, App-uh-LATCH-un) their mystery and lore have had an impact on my life. As a descendant of the infamous feuding McCoy family of Kentucky, I grew up hearing the old mountain tales, and through them came to understand something of the character of these hearty folk who let nothing come between them and their clans. A favorite story of my Grandmother's recounts the first time she was taken to meet my Grandfather's family, shocked to find one of his siblings screaming in rage while chasing another sibling through the house with a butcher knife. The family ignored the scene, continuing to greet my Grandmother warmly, chatting as amicably to her as if nothing unusual was happening. Later my Grandfather told her that such expressions of temper were normal in his family, but he assured her that if anyone outside the family had been chasing after either of the combatants, then they all surely would have grabbed their own knives and gotten into the fray.

Before attending the University of Texas, I spent two years at a small liberal arts college in the foothills of the Blue Ridge Mountains. The location afforded me many opportunities to experience the breathtaking grandeur of the Appalachian Mountains for myself. Like most non-mountaineers, I took with me a score of preconceived ideas about what the region and its people were like. On one hand I assumed that, since it was the latter half of the twentieth century, nearly all the old customs had died out, replaced by the modern conveniences and mindsets of the times. On the other hand, I suppose I still expected to see bearded hillbillies lolling under shade trees, drinking home brew out of brown jugs marked XXX, unsure when and if the Civil War had ended. In only a few short months, nearly every notion I had about Appalachian life was turned upside down and inside out.

While there truly were places which had no running water or electricity, and where families carried on their lives much as their ancestors had a century before, the total picture was a confusing mix of old and new. At some family gatherings women really did feed their men first, then stand back and wait their turn, but afterward they would all retire to the living room to watch television together. There really was a resistance to new ideas, usually discussed in the same conversation with the merits of college educations, new cars, and the coming computer age. Many of the young people really were possessed of remarkably strong bodies, the sort stereotypically seen on bad sitcoms. One young man I dated briefly could literally run up the side of a mountain without losing his breath, then stand there in disgust as I, on legs accustomed to the flat, rolling landscape of the midwest, huffed and puffed my way up after him.

I also found cities and towns which were not appreciably different from any other cities in the country. There are television stations, government buildings, large groceries, and the familiar chain stores where many other Americans regularly shop. The women wore the same clothing styles and the youth spoke much the same slang as other young people. I discovered what so many others have who venture into the mountains for the first time ... it is a land of deep contrast, where old and new do not so much blend as live side by side.

Television has helped feed our misbegotten fantasies about the backward ways of mountain folk through such popular offerings as "The Andy Griffith Show" (featuring the darkly superstitious Darling family, Barney Fife with his astounding fear of the paranormal, and the unbalanced Ernest T. Bass), "The Beverly Hillbillies" (who didn't even know what their doorbell or pool table were for), "The Waltons," and the latest offering, "Christy." Though the latter two certainly contain very realistic portrayals of the poverty and privations of the region, the first two were intended as comedic satires, and it was through these shows that an entire generation of Americans, myself included, first modeled their ideas about Appalachian people and their ways. In them, we are introduced to fearless, backward people who shun modern conveniences and inventions. They have little formal education, yet they possess a remarkable inner wisdom. We watch, laughing as they fail to grasp the intricacies of modern social interactions, but we know in the end that their simple wisdom will win out and it will be the flatlanders—the city slickers—who end up looking foolish.

About the only truth among all the stereotyping is the primitive conditions of the region which survived far into the twentieth century. Poverty was, and is, still keenly felt here, and an alarming number of mountain families earn incomes far below the poverty line.[5] This condition came about partly because of the characteristic resistance to change common in these people who have lived apart from the mainstream for so long, and partly because the rest of the world was blissfully unaware of their dire circumstances until long after World War II. Even when this awareness did emerge, there was a large and vocal contingent who assumed that there must be some native lack of ability in these folk who occasionally seemed to outsiders to be lazy and without ambition. How such conclusions were drawn about a people who still hunted their own food, wove their own cloth, and accomplished virtually every other facet of day-to-day life in the old and hard ways of their ancestors is a mystery.

These blue hills and their people, isolated for so long in a region which was largely impenetrable until fairly recently, simply did not receive the benefits of modernization the rest of the country enjoyed throughout the nineteenth century. While we may express ambivalent feelings about the concept of progress, in the case of southern Appalachia, these amenities included common commodities the rest of the country often took for granted—like schools and roads! In the first half of this century, mission schools were established to teach the mountain children, who had been discovered to be largely illiterate. Though these youngsters had little knowledge of the outside world, intelligence tests administered to them showed, overall, an above average intellect.[6] Therefore it amazed the teachers and ministers all the more that the mountain people tenaciously clung to their old ways. Particularly vexing was their refusal to give up their magickal practices and beliefs, which the missionaries blamed for holding back progress in the region.

Despite the efforts of the missionaries, the region retained both its "superstitious nonsense" and its poverty. The famous "moonshiners" (called "blockaders" in the mountains), named because they manufactured their corn whiskey under the cover of darkness (an art learned by their Celtic ancestors in Scotland and northern Ireland), were the only ones who were making more than a subsistence income by the 1920s.

The first really big change for Appalachia was the creation of the Tennessee Valley Authority, a federal corporation created by Congress in 1933. Still a powerful entity today, the TVA's dams harnessed the power of the vast Tennessee River to bring electricity to remote regions of Appalachia where it had never been before. This was an important first step in bringing the mountains into the twentieth century. The TVA also improved navigation and helped control flooding over a 41,000 square mile region, almost half of it in the mountains.

By the 1930s, roads had been built into most of the larger communities, and the coal mining and lumber industries were making some inroads into the poverty and isolation of the region. These industries employed fewer of the native mountaineers than was needed to relieve economic hardship, and did more to exploit and destroy the land than they did to bring any good to the needy. Growth projections focused on instant profit rather than on long-term impact to the region, and on profits in the pockets of distant corporate giants rather than in the pockets of those who performed the labor. No effort was made to put back into the land what was stripped from it, nor was money spent on environmental protection. As a result, some of the Appalachian rivers are now among the most dangerously polluted on the planet.[7]

President Franklin Roosevelt was the first government official to attempt to address the problem, but his earliest efforts were hampered by the more immediate problem of the Great Depression. In 1936, when the worst of the Depression had passed, Roosevelt and Congress decided that nationalizing large tracts of mountain land was the best way to address the issue. First they set aside a massive amount of acreage for the creation of the Cherokee National Forest, and in 1940 declared another 485,000 acres of wild mountain area in Tennessee and North Carolina be used for the creation of the Great Smoky Mountains National Park.[8] Other public projects followed over the decades: The Blue Ridge Parkway; The Appalachian Trail; The Cumberland State Park; The Peaks of Otter State Park; The Jefferson, Pisgah, and Washington National Forests, etc.; but—again—little benefit came to the people of the region through these projects. Most folks who lived on the newly nationalized property were forced to move from land on which they and their ancestors had lived for nearly two hundred years, and more than a few deadly battles with federal agents ensued.[9] Others lost their livelihoods along with the land, and were forced to go on federal relief programs or to move into government housing projects with their neighbors.[10]

In the 1950s, at a time when most of the nation was enjoying unprecedented prosperity, there seemed to be an assumption in Washington that the economy must be healthy in Appalachia as well, that their earlier bandage programs had somehow solved a long and deep-rooted problem.

In December of 1961, broadcast journalist Charles Kerault went on television with a heart-wrenching documentary called "Christmas in Appalachia." For the first time, Americans saw firsthand just how miserable conditions in the mountains were.[11] The program treated Americans to visions of children trudging barefoot in the snow, homes with only a fireplace for heat, drinking water contaminated by livestock, and diseases which the rest of the country had thought eradicated running rampant like the plague though mountain communities. For the first time, the country as a whole reacted, and over the next decade many social programs were created which attempted not only to ease the deprivation in Appalachia, but to gently bring its inhabitants into the twentieth century as well. Programs such as VISTA (Volunteers in Service to America) attracted hundreds of eager young people. True to our television image of the hillbilly winning out over the city slicker, reports filed by many of these adventurers show that they learned as much as they taught, and felt rewarded by the experience of getting to know the mountaineers.[12]

If the old adage that "in all evil there lies a core of good" holds true, this can certainly be seen in the history of Appalachia. For those of us interested in preserving and reinstating the magickal practices and wisdom of the common people, the isolation which created this poverty also left us a unique pocket of ancient ways, little touched until recent times by the modern world. Some sociologists are fond of saying that the twentieth century did not arrive in Appalachia until sometime around 1980. Sadly, with this progress has come the decimation of an old way of life, with little increase in quality of life to show for the effort. Like much of the rest of the planet, the Appalachians—both the land and its culture—continue today to be raped in the name of progress.

The 1980s and '90s have seen a renewed interest in the folkways of the American people in general, and of Appalachia in particular. Many of the old ways have been collected, written down, and preserved for us by students and teachers of folklore, and by the curious onlooker. Unfortunately, others have been lost to us, as the last generation to have practiced them on a daily basis continues to die out. If we look closely at Appalachian customs we find that many of the old magickal ways are still alive and well—or at least not completely forgotten—and in recreating those ways, we can gain new insights into our common European heritage.

We magickal folk must hurry in our quest to gather up the remnants of the Appalachian past. Modern life is destroying the old ways faster than we can relearn them. Hand-crafted items are being discarded in favor of factory-made gear. Cable television is leaving the storyteller's art behind and decimating regional accents which, until very recently, still kept many of the words and inflections of eighteenth-century Scotland and England. The old magickal ways are being scoffed at more and more by a younger generation, whose hearts, like those of other young Americans, are set on a future of making money and achieving fame. The new generation is more interested in modern music than their native ballads, pop stars rather than folk heroes, and the movies rather than storytelling. Sadly, there is little time for magick anymore, even in these ancient blue mountains which have so kindly preserved and cherished it for us.

Endnotes to Introduction

1. Porter, Elliot. *Appalachian Wilderness: The Great Smoky Mountains* (New York: Ballantine Books, 1973).
2. Ibid, p. 55.
3. Ibid.
4. Ibid, p. 56.
5. Caudill, Harry M. *Night Comes to the Cumberlands: A Biography of a Depressed Area* (Boston: Little, Brown and Co., 1962).
6. Peattie, Roderick, ed. *The Great Smokies and the Blue Ridge* (New York: Vanguard Press, 1943).
7. Caudill.
8. Ibid.
9. Almost any period newspaper from the region will illustrate this point. Also see Caudill.
10. Caudill.
11. Ibid.
12. Some of these accounts are related in the *Foxfire* series of books,

others in folklore journals (listed in Bibliography). Those interested in more detailed accounts might wish to consult the VISTA archives at the Library of Congress.

13. Some magickians feel there are dangers inherent in any form of graveyard magick, and they tailor their spells accordingly. Please refer to Chapter Eight ("Integrating Appalachian Folk Magick With Your Own Magickal Lifestyle") for full discussion, and instructions for altering the spells found in this book to suit your needs and magickal beliefs.

CHAPTER ONE

Folk Magick and the Mountains

There's an old spinning wheel in the corner,
Spinning tales of the long, long ago,
The wheel turns and out comes a story,
The tale of a girl and her beau.
    —Traditional Mountain Ballad

The term "folk magick," like its cousins: "folklore," "folkway," "folk belief," etc., has a very nebulous definition. Sometimes referred to as "low magick," folk magick was—and still is—the magickal practices of the common people. They are the spells, incantations, and daily rituals known throughout clans and communities which have been handed down orally from one generation to another. Like a gentle river, the magick has subtly changed with each generation as it flows into new hands. New interpretations have been placed upon it, new twists added to old formulae—but always, at heart, it has remained the same—a living testimony to the spiritual and cosmological beliefs of those who came before us.

Folk magick does not—nor did it ever—require a lot of elaborate preparation, expensive tools, specialized knowledge, or the assistance of someone from a priestly caste to beseech the aid of distant deities. Unlike ceremonial magick, often referred to as "high magick," it does not demand years of training and self-discipline, it does not command otherworldly entities to do its bidding, nor does it exist in a fixed form which must be slavishly adhered to in order to be successful.[1] Because it does not require allegiance to any one creed or concept of divinity, it can be used by anyone who feels it to be useful. While certain principles must be applied to the magickal practices—the same basic ones which make all types of spells work—folk magick is a living thing, ever changing and growing with the needs of the people it serves.

A broader, and perhaps more modern, interpretation would class folk magick as the beliefs and practices of a single culture or locale which concerns itself with bringing about desired changes by performing acts seemingly unrelated to the hoped-for outcome. For some, such as those in the modern-day magickal community, there is no differentiation between folk magick and personal lifestyle. For others, the practices of folk magick are viewed as no more than mere superstition, the ancient remnants of an unenlightened past being visited upon the ignorant and gullible.

The flaw in this last definition is that it starts from a prejudiced position, one which assumes *urdummheit* on the part of the followers of folk magickal ways. Urdummheit is a German word meaning "primeval stupidity," the arrogant and often false assumption that those who lived before us, or who live elsewhere, or who follow older traditions or faiths, are somehow inherently less intelligent. Yet when we drop our prejudices and expand our thinking to include the entire 360-degree circumference of existence, one spiritual truth becomes evident: one person's superstition is another's truth, and one's heresy is another's faith.

The word "superstition" literally means "struck paralyzed with awe," and was once used in religious circles when referring to miraculous occurrences of a divine nature. It wasn't until the eighteenth century that the term superstition was applied to magickal practices and other folk ways, and thus was degraded in meaning just as it sought to degrade that to which it was applied. All omens, rituals, spiritual beliefs, and concepts of divinity can and have been at times classed as "just" superstitions by someone else purveying a different worldview. Virtually all of these things were at one time part of the folk magick of the people from whose culture they came, even those which became codified into the basic tenets of the world's major religions.

To understand the folk magick of a people is to understand that people's history, for they are inextricably linked. Their magick provides a window to the past which allows us to look at things as they once were, and helps us to glean a greater understanding of the spiritual practices, thought processes, and cosmological concepts of our ancestors. This is especially important for those who are interested in the art of magick itself, and who wish to bring it into common practice again.

Folk Magick in Appalachia

Appalachian folk magick primarily concerns omens, portents, curses, cures, and protections, and is decidedly geared to non-material goals, a consequence which at first seems out of place in a region which has had so little of the basics of life. Yet in this place where shoes and secure homes have been luxury items, spells for money, food, shelter, or clothing are virtually non-existent. Instead the magick focuses on intangible values: family and home, romance and children, health and dying. When "prosperity" is mentioned as the goal of an Appalachian spell, it refers to an overall quality of life rather than monetary well-being. To the mountain people, you are considered prosperous if you have the love of friends and family, a roof over your head, food on the table, and a means of making a living, regardless of income level.

When attempting to root out the folk magick of any culture, we must go to what is often our only remaining primary source—the folk stories told for generations around the fireplaces at night.[2] Because Appalachian traditions have been preserved orally, storytelling and ballad making was—and still is—a valued art, just as it was to their Celtic ancestors. It is from the legends and folk songs of any people that we learn of their magickal ways. When we read or listen with hope of discovering a pattern, one usually emerges which obligingly points the way. This is the same way in which modern Pagans, followers of old earth religions, find insight into the ancient ways of their ancestors, and it is still our most reliable method for collecting data from the unrecorded past. Because this is the best, sometimes the only source available, the process of collecting magickal practices can be painstaking, as they are often found "buried" in other works whose compilers were probably unaware that they recorded magick. These remnants need be extracted with a keen eye and re-pieced into a workable system.

The Roots of Appalachian Folk Magick

By the early nineteenth century, relations between the Cherokee and the Europeans were on very friendly terms, with a great deal of intermarriage between the two diverse groups. The legendary statesman and Republic of Texas President, Sam Houston, was one of many men who took a Cherokee bride (however, her father was a Scottish immigrant), and by the time the government of Georgia sent the Cherokee west to Oklahoma territory (in 1835), along what has become known as the Trail of Tears, it is estimated that more than half of those banished were at least one-quarter European. Hence, some of the folk magick of Appalachia, particularly folk healing, reflects Native American roots.[3]

The first Europeans to settle in the mountains came in the mid-eighteenth century when most of the rest of the North American population was hugging the Atlantic coastline. The earliest of these came in the late 1740s. In 1745, the Highland clans fought

West Virginia

Kentucky

Cumberland Mountains

Virginia

Tennessee

Great Smoky Mountains

Blue Ridge Mountains

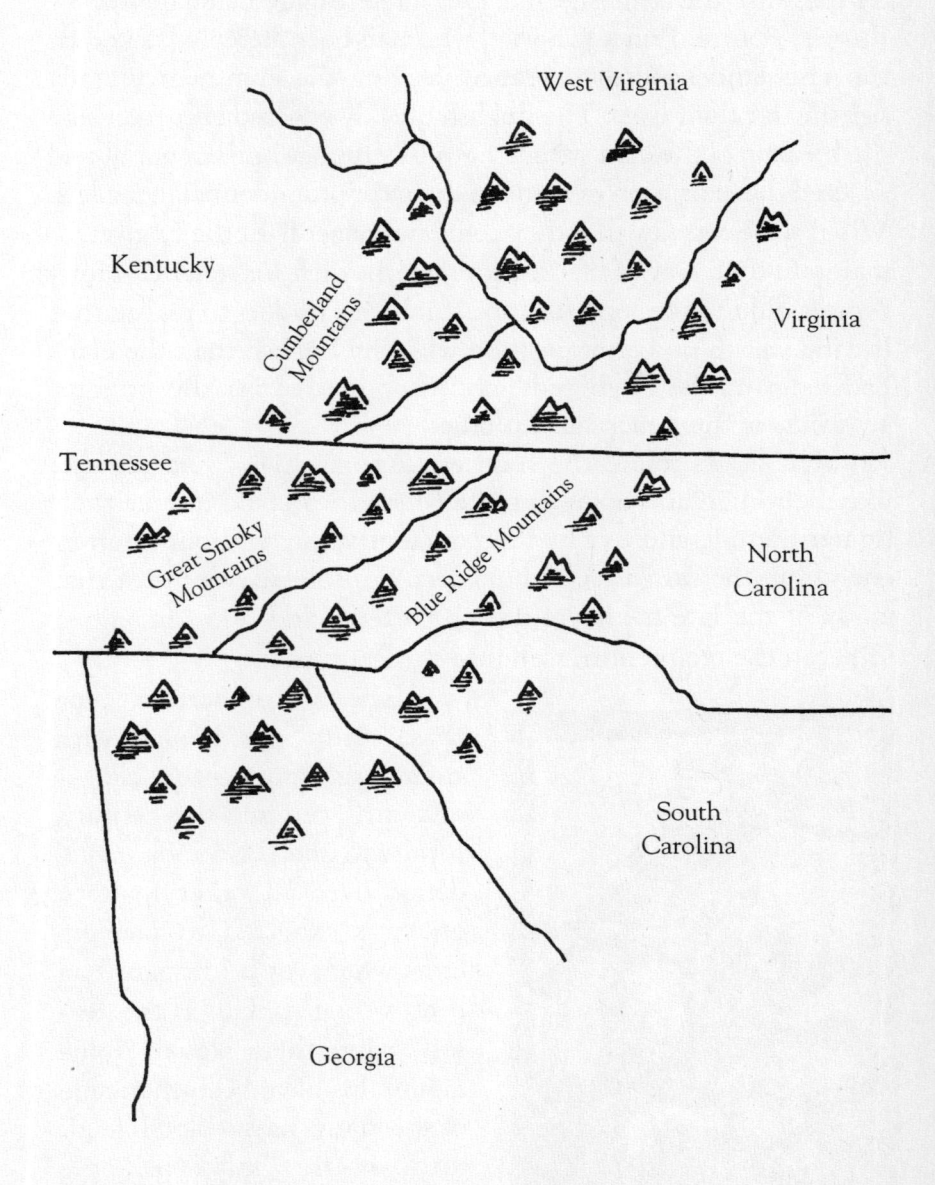

North Carolina

South Carolina

Georgia

The Heart of Appalachia

their last great battle at Culloden Field to maintain their clan system against the English, and lost.⁴ The Stuart claimant to the throne, Bonnie Prince Charlie, who had been fiercely backed by the Highlanders, fled to France, leaving the clansmen literally fighting for their lives. The English quickly enacted laws to ensure the breakup of the clan system, both its structure and economy, and ordered the execution of many of the most prominent clan leaders. When the Scots saw that they could no longer fight the English, or maintain their way of life in Scotland, they left for Ireland.⁵ However, it didn't take long for the astute clan leaders to realize that Ireland was in no better position with the English than the clans had been in the Highlands, and they headed for the brighter prospects of the American Colonies.

The Scots found the southern Appalachians very remote, like their Highland home, a place where they could resume their former lifestyle and live by their ancient values without interference from the *sassenach*, or outsiders. So isolated were they that many of the late medieval speech patterns and terms remained intact in the region until well into this century.⁶

The most important value these hearty Scots brought with them was family—the clan—and until well into this century, loyalty to one's clan took precedence over all other matters; one was expected to take up arms whenever a kinsman had been wronged. This is the reason why these lovely blue mountains have been the scene of so many nasty blood feuds such as the infamous ones between the Hatfields and the McCoys, and the Martins and the Tollivers.⁷

The other Europeans who came to settle in the mountains were largely slum dwellers from London, Liverpool, and Dublin, who fled both poverty and the hangman's noose.[8] Decidedly less educated and polished than their Scottish neighbors, these immigrants knew how to live by their wits, how to flee the law, and how to make do with very little—skills they would need to survive in the harsh Appalachians.

Both of these groups brought with them to the mountains the simple folklore and magick of early eighteenth-century Scotland, Ireland, and England, practices which reflected the medieval beliefs of their homelands, and which in turn had roots in the pre-Christian Pagan spiritualities of western Europe. Those with working knowledge of Anglo-Celtic magick will easily be able to see these roots in the spells of Appalachia, though it will also be clear that mountain magick has developed its own earmarked traits over the centuries, ones often at variance with modern Pagan magickal practices.[9] The specific characteristics usually found in mountain magickal practices and folk beliefs are:

1. A division of all that exists into distinct and warring camps of good and evil.
2. A sense that all things have their own sentient quality, be they plant, animal, or inanimate object, and that their intent for good or evil can be made manifest.
3. A strong belief in the influence of the Christian Devil.
4. An acceptance that magick is real and that it can be worked for either good or evil purposes.
5. The belief that certain individuals are blessed with paranormal powers and that their magick is always more powerful than that of the layperson.
6. A sense of fatalism in the face of certain dire circumstances, particularly during severe illness or intrusion by outsiders into the local way of life, conditions which no amount of magick can completely cure. (Fatalist thinking is the first cousin of

predestination, a spiritual legacy left to the mountain people through the Calvinist theology prevalent in the early Scottish Protestant churches.)

7. That the resting places of the dead are places wherein evil may lurk, but which contain great magickal powers which can be harnessed by the brave.

8. An underlying magickal philosophy which says it is wicked to work magick for monetary profit or to gain power over another individual, though the latter condition is frequently ignored, especially in matters of romance or inter-family quarrels.

9. The acceptance of the reality and potency of magickal curses.

10. The belief that nature provides omens and portents of the future, and these are to be heeded by the wise.

11. An emphasis upon actions, rather than upon thought and willpower, as the ultimate magickal catalyst.

About Appalachian "Witches"

Contrary to popular misconceptions which have been handed down to us from the middle ages, Witches are not depraved humans who have sold their souls to the Christian Satan. A Witch is not a doer of evil, but is by definition a Pagan, a follower of any one of the many old nature religions which are being revived all over the planet. These religions, often collectively called Witchcraft, have no Satan, no single authority, and their adherents acknowledge many different deities. Like the followers of other religions, Witchcraft seeks above all else to unite worshippers with their deity(ies) and to seek their will. Witchcraft is a positive, loving, life-affirming spirituality with many faces, whose practitioners (of which I am proudly one) fight daily battles for acceptance and understanding in an unenlightened world which still cowers in fear at the word "Witch."

Because Witch is the label for the follower of a specific religious tradition (like a Jew, Christian, or Moslem) I generally prefer that the word be capitalized just like any other proper noun.

However, in this text it will appear in lowercase. I do this to differentiate between the mountain folk's concept of a witch and a religious Witch.

In Appalachia, neither the medieval definition of witches as hags cavorting with Satan, nor the reclaimed identity of those following the nature religions, is an accurate one. In these misty blue mountains, a witch is as likely as not to be a fellow member of the local fundamentalist church, or a loner who gathers herbs at midnight under a full moon to make healing brews, and who worships his God alone in his cabin. For the most part, the old Gods and Goddesses of Europe have been long forgotten by these folk, and one finds that they may call upon either the Judeo-Christian God or the Devil to assist in their spells without pledging allegiance to either. Those who are called "witch" by their neighbors suffer little if any ridicule or harm as long as the community is aware of the practice and has been shown benefits. The communities see these eccentrics as fulfilling a vital need in the community and, though they may be tempted to say a protective prayer as they walk past a witch's cabin, they would not want to be without their wise folk.

Part of this curious acceptance of witchcraft in an area known for its hearty strain of religious fundamentalism can again be traced to the Anglo-Celtic roots of the people. Unlike in Catholic Europe where the crime of witchcraft was one against God and the Church, a breech of ecclesiastical law, in Britain it was a civil crime, one which was merely defined as doing harm to others (known as *malefica,* a Latin term meaning "bad deed") and violating the "King's Peace."[10] The Scottish Highlanders who fled to preserve their old Celtic ways brought with them the attitude that magick is by and large natural, whether or not we always understand why and how it works. Belief in magick as part of religious practice was an accepted part of everyday life to the Pagan Celts, and its practice flourished openly for many centuries, into the common era.[11]

Like Pagan Witches, the mountain witches often use the power of the four cardinal directions, and the native herbs and roots of their land, to enhance their magick. Both males and females wear the label and both are called upon to heal the sick, dispense love potions, change the weather, protect neighbors from ghosts, bless hunts, deliver babies, and teach the old ways to willing youngsters. Appalachian witches tend to be older people, if not elderly, and seem gifted with a certain amount of psychic power. They most often come from witch families whose talents have been noted and well-regarded for generations, and are usually looked up to with a curious mixture of respect and caution.

Witches are believed able to know things which they have never witnessed, and to be capable of working their magick from a great distance, though being in the same locale certainly promotes stronger magick. Distance is rarely a problem for the skilled witch, and mountain folk accept that certain witches can enter their homes "in spirit" (by passing through walls) to gain information, to heal, or to level curses.[12] Even the less powerful witches are believed to be able to pass into homes through keyholes and chimneys, entrances which are magickally guarded in mountain homes, just as they were in old Europe. These beliefs have firm roots in a hard-to-master art known as astral projection, the practice of sending one's consciousness forth to remote locations.

The only time witches seem to pose a problem to the community is if one is practicing witchcraft unknown to his or her neighbors. These people are thought to be up to no good and are avoided if possible. There is a mountain custom which says that nothing which you personally own should ever be handed over to someone you suspect of being a secret witch, lest they use the item to curse you.

When the people of the mountains need magickal assistance which they feel lies beyond their own abilities, the local witch is often called upon for help. Modern Witches take note that, in keeping with the ancient ways, these witches do not charge for their services, but graciously accept what is offered as a token of appreciation.

Granny Women, Water Witches, and Storytellers

Three types of specific magickal folk who still have a thriving and open practice in the Appalachian Mountains today are granny women, water witches, and storytellers.

As the title suggests, granny women are always female, usually elder members of the community. The closest analogous term we have for them is "midwives," but the granny women of Appalachia are so much more than the deliverers of babies. Granny women above all else possess ancient herbal knowledge of the land. They know how to concoct poultices, teas, and other remedies to ease —if not fully cure—most of the ailments common to their people. In a region which has been long-noted for its distrust of modern medicine, it is often the granny women who are first consulted as to what cure to take. The recipe for the cure is as likely to include magickal actions as it is medicinal ones.

Most of the granny women are believed to possess second sight, and their predictions, traditionally given at Christmas or the New Year, are listened to carefully and heeded well. The fact that the traditional time for her prophecies is near the winter solstice is a certain carry-over from Pagan divination customs which were also commonly practiced at this time of year.

Granny women are also believed to be able to see into the character of a person's soul, and thus they are often asked to bestow a name on the children they deliver. This is a survival of another Celtic custom wherein the clan chieftain or high priest would be asked to give the proper name to a new life.

Water witches are more commonly known in other parts of the English speaking world as "dowsers."[13] These are people who are able to find wells, underground creeks and springs, and other hidden water sources by the use of a two-handled rod. While many excellent female dowsers abound, in Appalachia this is a trade which is almost exclusively male. In a region where many of the folk must still rely on private wells and springs as their only water source, the water witch provides a vital function in locating the best place(s) to sink a well or lay down costly pipes and pumps, saving the owners of the land much money in drilling expenses.

The mountains seem to possess an inordinate amount of highly skilled water witches, most of whom appear to have inherited their gift from a father or grandfather. Testing done by curious and independent parties from outside of the mountains has documented the remarkable skills of these men who have been able to accurately follow a meandering trail of underground water pipes specifically laid down in an effort to thwart them.

Each water witch has his own technique for discovering water, but all involve the use of a dowsing rod, a wooden or metal tool crafted by the dowser which best resembles a long slingshot. Holding on to the two pronged ends, the water witch walks slowly across the land where water is being sought and waits for some sign from his rod that he is near or over a source. In some cases, the rod will wobble from side to side, in others it will point straight down. Like a modern geiger counter, the amount of activity or movement attests to the quantity and nearness of the hidden water source.

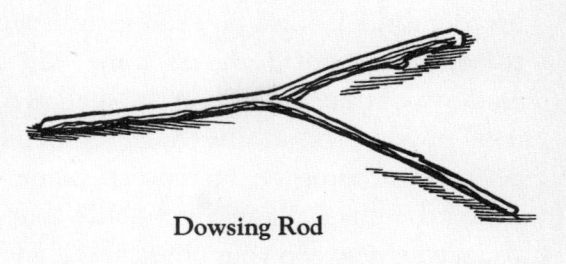

Dowsing Rod

Though bookstores and television have made deep inroads into the rural life of the mountaineers in the past ten years, the storyteller is still a valued part of the more isolated communities, though his or her function as the keeper of the community's traditions and history is rapidly fading. In the not-too-distant past, the storyteller was a featured entertainment at all mountain gatherings. After the dancing, drinking, and feasting was done, folks would gather around the fires to hear the folktales of the mountains being retold. "Haint" tales, or ghost stories, were favored by the youngsters, and the adults liked the historical tales of their clans or of the people who lived in the mountains before them. Often the communal enjoyment of a familiar story staved off hot tempers between families which had been quarreling. In any case, the taller and more embellished the story, the better![14]

In the role of the storyteller it is easy to see the deep, unbroken link to the mountain peoples' Celtic heritage. In Scotland, the itinerant storytellers were often traveling bards who also kept the traditions and mythology of their people alive and provided entertainment on long quiet nights. These weavers of words, called *senachies* in Gaelic, still ply their trade at festivals and fairs throughout modern Scotland and Ireland.

Making Appalachian Folk Magick Work for You

The folk spells found in this book can work for just one reason ... because the magickian wants them badly enough to make them work. As any magickal person can tell you, desire and need is the driving force behind any successful spell. The desire, your emotional investment in the outcome, will propel you to spend great amounts of time visualizing the spell as manifest. In terms of magickal physics, this means that your mental vision has brought the desire into being on an unseen plane of existence, sometimes called the astral plane. Eventually that sympathetic energy link you create between your physical self and the unseen creation will draw it into the physical world.

If you are unfamiliar with the workings of magick, begin by following the ten steps listed below when working any of the spells in this, or virtually any other book on natural magick:

1. Have a clear desire or need for something which you can put both into simple words and mental pictures.

2. Build your emotional investment in the outcome of the spell by spending as much time as you can visualizing it as manifest in your life.

3. Decide if the spell is ethical (discussed in detail later in this chapter), or if it will bring harm to others.

4. Smile a lot as you think about your spell, or laugh or dance ... whatever you think of as an expression of joy. Magick should be fun, and being solemn too often can only work against you in the long run. Old magickal wisdom tells us that expressions of overt joy in the face of disaster will often turn the balance in our favor.

5. Gather whatever items you will need for the spell itself, handling them often as you visualize so that your energy and need become a part of these tools. This is called charging or enchanting the items. These will not work the magick for you, but will act as a catalyst or focus for your magick and, as such, are very important.

6. Plan the time and place of the spell to suit your lifestyle, and to incorporate any special timing preferences you have, such as

working spells on the new moon, on a Sunday, at dawn, etc. Keep in mind that privacy for concentration is essential and that certain demands on your time may force you to deviate from the traditional timing of the spell. For instance, if you work nights, then getting up to do a spell at dawn is exhausting and counterproductive. A well-rested magickian who is alert and focused always makes the best magick, regardless of when the spell is cast.

7. Work the actual spell at least once, but be willing to repeat it as often as needed with all the energy and devotion you put into the first working.

8. Be willing to experiment with new wording in your spells (often referred to as words of power), herb or stone substitutions, new locations, a different time of day, etc. Sometimes small changes that feel right to you can make a big difference.

9. When you are finished, know on all levels of your being that your magickal operation has indeed caused the need to manifest on an unseen plane of existence and that it is only a matter of time before it comes into your physical life. So much of successful magick is based on the magickian's own mental perception, and so this belief is crucial to the outcome.

10. Have the ability to keep silent about your magickal work.

Keeping silent about magickal work is a medieval belief which may have stemmed partly from fear of discovery by witch hunters, but in ancient times it was probably linked to an old adage which teaches that energy divided is energy lost. In other words, the more you speak to others of your work, the more energy you lose which could otherwise be channeled into your desired outcome. Then there is always a chance you may also find yourself talking to someone who does not believe in the power of magick, or who is jealous of your magickal successes, or—worse yet—has some vested interest in your failure. Such people can seriously impair your magick with their destructive counter-energy. Never mind that they do not believe in what you are doing, we all have the power to project energy, and negative mental output will still work against you.

Magickal Ethics and Appalachian Folk Spells

Modern Witches (yes, this time with a capital W) have few rules and laws, but there is one which is almost a universal, and that is a law against doing any magick which will harm or manipulate another living being. They accept the fact that any harm they unleash will be revisited upon them three times over, making the exercise not only pointless, but dangerous as well.

In Appalachian folk magick, there are many spells which cross that line. A good number of these are presented in this text simply because they encompass so large a part of the extant magick of the region. The reader is encouraged to use his or her own good judgment as to the degree of harm the spell might wreak on others and to either avoid the spell, or modify it to negate its manipulative clauses. This can be as simple as adding a line to the spell stating, "as it harms none," "for the good of all concerned," "in accordance with free will," or "as each may will it to be," while visualizing this concept of "harm none" as part of the finished spell.

There are also a goodly number of spells and practices which use animals in ways which could be interpreted as abusive. While my own ethics dictate that I may not harm animals in my magick, many other magickians feel differently and have made thought-provoking intellectual arguments in the defense of their practices. Please understand that this book in no way advocates harming any animal for magickal purposes, but because these practices make up a fair portion of Appalachian folk magick they are included here. You will have to look into your own heart to decide for yourself how best to proceed when the life or well-being of an animal is at stake.

If you feel too involved with your magickal need to be objective about it (something which is all too easy to do), you don't have to rely solely on your own intuition about its outcome. One of the most time-honored ways of deciding whether a spell is harmless or not is to perform some sort of divination prior to the working. Tarot cards, runes, casting lots, looking for signs, vision questing, pendulum use, etc., have all been employed to this end. If you do not already have a method of divination which works for you, you may want to check into some of the practical books on these topics which can easily be found in your local library or bookstore. If you are already proficient in at least one method of divination, simply ask the oracle to provide you with an overview of all the possible ramifications of the spell as it now stands. If the oracle does indicate a troubling area, try rewriting the words of the spell or modifying the intent somewhat to see if this changes the potential outcome. Sometimes these simple changes are all you need to avoid unintentionally hurting someone—possibly even yourself! If you make changes but still cannot get a divination outcome with which you are comfortable, perhaps you ought to rethink your need for the spell. Only you can make the final decision, since you are the one who will have to live with the consequences of the outcome.

Endnotes to Chapter 1

1. Details of the complex practices of ceremonial magick lie beyond the scope of this book. For those interested in a solid, basic primer on the subject, one with practical material as well, I suggest looking into Donald Michael Kraig's *Modern Magick: Eleven Lessons in the High Magickal Arts* (Llewellyn, 1988).

2. Brunvand, Jan H. *The Study of American Folklore: An Introduction* (New York: W. W. Norton, Co., 1986), third edition.

3. Hutchens, Alma R. *Indian Herbalogy of North America* (Windsor, ON: Merco [fifteenth edition], 1989).

4. McLynn, Frank. *The Jacobites* (New York: Routledge and Kegan Paul, Inc., 1985).

5. Ford, Henry J. *The Scotch-Irish in America* (Princeton, NJ: Princeton University Press, 1915).

6. Peattie, Roderick, ed. *The Great Smokies and the Blue Ridge*, Introduction (New York: Vanguard Press, 1943).

7. Jones, Virgil Carrington. *The Hatfields and the McCoys* (Chapel Hill: The University of North Carolina Press [sixth printing], 1979).

8. Ford, pp. 22–37.

9. Anglo-Celtic magickal practices and beliefs are numerous and complex, but can be gleaned from the following texts: Conway, D. J. *Celtic Magic* (St. Paul, MN: Llewellyn Worldwide, 1990). McCoy, Edain. *Celtic Myth and Magick* (St. Paul, MN: Llewellyn Worldwide, 1995). Matthews, John. *The Celtic Shaman* (Shaftesbury, Dorset: Element Books, 1991). Rees, Alwyn, and Brinley Rees. *Celtic Heritage* (London: Thames and Hudson [second printing], 1989).

10. This "lax" attitude toward the paranormal infuriated the Puritans, an early brand of Christian fundamentalists, who viewed any type of magick or deviation from strict Biblical teaching as Devilment. These dissenters also fled to the New World and settled in New England where, in 1692, their hysteria and intolerance blossomed into the infamous Salem witch trials during which dozens of innocent people were hanged for their "crimes."

11. Ross, Anne. *Everyday Life of the Pagan Celts* (New York: G. P. Putman's Sons, 1970).

12. Wigginton, Eliot, ed. *Foxfire 2* (Garden City, NY: Doubleday and Co., 1973.)

13. The history and mechanics of dowsing can be found in Joseph Baum's *The Beginner's Handbook of Dowsing* (Crown Publishers, Inc., 1974). A complete discussion of Appalachian dowsing practices and beliefs is outlined in *Foxfire 2*.

14. The Appalachian people's love of tall tales can be confirmed through many sources, all of which make entertaining reading. See the Bibliography for specific titles.

CHAPTER TWO

Death, Dying, and "Haints"

Down by the weeping willow
Where the violets are in bloom,
There lies a fair young maiden
All silent in her tomb.
　　　　　—Traditional Mountain Song

Perhaps no subject has been the object of such deep fascination for the mountain folks as death, dying, and the afterlife. This preoccupation has been noted and documented by both sociologists and folklorists, and thus we have a rich body of lore in which to rediscover this aspect of folk magick.[1]

Of Lyches and the Graveyard

Much magick concerning personal protection and one's own longevity centers around the cemetery and the "lych," an Old English word for "corpse," which is still commonly used in the southern mountains. As the use of this term would suggest, Appalachian death customs closely resemble those of the British Isles during the late medieval period.[2] Although many of these old ways have faded out in the last half-century, to be replaced by the death customs followed in other Christian communities around the country, one can still occasionally find an isolated pocket or two which adheres to the old practices.

When there is a large bell available, such as a church bell, it is tolled to announce a death in the family. Traditionally the number of rings is indicative of the age of the deceased.[3] This way friends and family living in other parts of the community not only know that a death has occurred, but the bell count may also tell them who died. This practice is a carry-over from old England where communal bells were frequently rung at times of transition—death, the end of the harvest, start of a battle, etc. Bells were also used in Britain and Ireland to chase away ghosts, evil spirits, and faeries who might be lurking around, especially those attracted to funeral rites.[4]

As soon as the death occurs, all reflective surfaces, especially mirrors, are covered, and all clocks or watches in the house stopped. Both of these things are considered bad luck to have in a house wherein lies a corpse, and it is believed that leaving these tasks undone will only bring further deaths to the family. Since mirrors have always been magickally viewed as portals to other worlds of existence, this belief may be rooted in the fear of seeing the spirit of the recently dead person peering back. The association of clocks with the life expectancy of a human being can be dated to the medieval period.[5] The old and familiar children's folk song which tells us that the grandfather clock, "stopped, short, never to run again, when the old man died" preserves for us this belief. Looking in mirrors and enjoying the convenience of timepieces must be avoided until after the funeral.

The first step in preparing the body is to dig up any severed body parts which are buried nearby. For a long time it was believed that a person had to be buried whole in order to be resurrected during the last days of the earth, as prophesied in fundamentalist Christianity, but this practice probably dates back to the time of the Celtic warrior chieftains who were also buried whole so that they would be able to fight at full capacity when they rose again to defend their country and clan. Belief in these guardian warriors was quite prevalent in old Britain, and we can find excellent examples of this echoed in the myths of King Arthur of Camelot, whom Celtic myth says will one day return to the throne when his country needs him most.

The casket, usually made of native wood by the family, is traditionally lined with black for an adult and white for a child. Often sweet-smelling herbs such as mountain woodruff are tossed inside, both as a practical measure against odors and as a gesture of ritual blessing—another carry-over from a Pagan past.

If this idea of a final blessing appeals to you, simply arrange to have some private time alone with the open casket. Strew the herbs over the body while offering your wishes aloud. These can be tailored to fit any need, or spiritual tradition. For instance, you may wish the person a speedy trip to the land of the dead (Heaven, Tir-na-nog, Avalon, etc.), so you might say something like the words on the next page.

On wings of air, may your spirit soar,
Onward and upward, evermore—
To find at last that joyous rest,
In the arms of (insert name of deity),
Your soul be blessed.

Or you might want to request that the departed soul reincarnate with you again in this life:

Into the Otherworld, riding on love
Which I sent to you on your journey above.
Don't leave me lonely through my earthly trial,
Rejoin me, if you will, and stay a while.

Soon after death, the lych is dressed as elaborately as the family's circumstances will allow, and laid out in his or her own home to await the wake. A wake is an old Irish custom which survives to this day in Ireland, as well as in the southern mountains. Family and friends of the deceased sit up all night with the body, not leaving it until the next day's procession to the cemetery. During this time no mourning is allowed, only the sharing of good memories about the deceased, and eating and drinking. The mountain folk believe, as the Irish do, that the spirit of the one passed over is still among them and enjoying the reminiscences as well. Often a glass of whiskey is poured for the deceased and placed near the body as an offering of hospitality.

The food and drink are believed to absorb any sins remaining with the person upon death. That night the plate is placed outdoors for the sin eater to consume. The sin eater lived in total isolation and supported himself (it was almost always a man) by eating the remains of these meals prepared for the dead or gravely ill. This gave the dying person absolution and guaranteed admission into heaven. The sin eater lived in total isolation, shunned by the rest of the community. They supported him because they felt they needed his services, but to come into contact with him was to risk absorbing the sins he had taken on. The practice comes from medieval Ireland, and was common in Appalachia until the early twentieth century.

Before the coffin is sealed, it is traditional for the family members and closest friends to file past to kiss the body, usually on the lips. The reasons for this were two-fold: first, it is an act of magick to ensure one's own long life, and second, if the deceased had been murdered there was a prevalent belief that the body would physically react to the touch of its murderer. The origin of the practice is rooted in Celtic beliefs about reincarnation which taught that rebirth would occur within one's own clan or tribe. It was customary to kiss persons as they died, particularly fallen warriors, so that their last breath would be "kept safe" for them by a member of their own clan, until they could return. This custom was practiced until the eighteenth century by Scottish Highland warriors, the direct ancestors of many of the Appalachian pioneers.

The last event before the coffin is nailed shut is for the oldest clan member to toss salt into it. In the folk magick of Europe, salt has enjoyed a long and honored history as a grounding element, one which channels energy into the earth and roots it there. Salt is also used liberally in spells for magickal protection, and it is likely that this custom may once have been a magickal effort to keep the lych's spirit in the ground where it belonged, and not running abroad in the night, startling loved ones.

Funerals usually take place in the graveyard rather than in churches, and the body must be carried there by the family and other mourners who have now ended their revelry and taken up mourning in earnest. Witnesses to mountain funerals are often astounded by the great outpouring of emotion—even hysterics—which characterize Appalachian funerals. The path to the cemetery is not always the most direct route, but traditionally follows a path known as a "funeral trail." Here again we see a remnant of burial customs from Scotland, where similar trails were once followed. The Scots believ-ed that certain types of unpleasant spirit life were attracted to the path of mourning, so the same route to the graveyard was likely used over and over again in an effort to confine them to one locale.

While along the funeral trail, certain omens foretell the fate of the family left behind. A snake crossing in front of a funeral procession is a very bad omen, often heralding future trouble with the lych's ghost. This is probably a bizarre twist of old Pagan belief wherein the snake represents regeneration and reincarnation. It is possible that this was misinterpreted to mean that the ghost would be coming back to visit periodically, rather than being reborn into the family. Coming across burrowing animals along the trail is a good omen, perhaps because of their association with the earth, and this omen may have originally indicated that the spirit of the deceased was not restless and would remain where he was put.

In Appalachia, the last person buried in the graveyard becomes its guardian spirit, until he or she is replaced by a new-comer. People traveling near a mountain graveyard, particularly at night, most fear seeing this specter who can be just as unpre-dictable, or as kind, as the last person interred there tended to be. Cemeteries are scrupulously avoided on the dark moon, a night when the guardian can, if he likes, choose to replace himself with anyone who happens by.

If you have to walk past a graveyard at a time considered dan-gerous, or if you feel uncomfortable doing so, there are magickal ways to protect yourself. At the edge of the cemetery, pick up a stone, carry it in your right hand until you have passed the bound-aries of the graveyard, then set the stone down without looking back and you may go on your way unharmed. The practice of leav-ing the site of a spell without looking back is not unknown in

Europe, though the many spells which carry this admonition in Appalachia probably have their roots in Biblical sources, primarily in the story of Lot's wife who refused to obey the command not to look back at the destruction of the city of Sodom, and was turned into a pillar of salt for her transgression.

If you know in advance that you will be walking near a cemetery, you can use the age-old protection of wearing some garlic cloves around your neck. (Haven't we all seen the *Dracula* movies?)

Omens of Death

Among the principal portents of death in Appalachia are birds, the precise meaning of their appearance indicated by either their location or behavior. This is of little surprise since, in Celtic mythology, birds symbolize the transition from the physical realm to an Otherworldly existence, particularly when a person finds him or herself magickally transformed into a bird.[6]

A bird flying into your house is a death omen which is still respected not only in the mountains, but in Britain and numerous other places as well. The symbolism at work here is clearly the idea of the bird flying away with the human soul. Unfortunately, no one has devised a way to overturn this ancient curse, and many have succumbed to it, more from fear than from any physical ailment which may ensue.

If a bird flies down and gets tangled in your hair, it is an indication that the bird has linked itself with your soul, and whatever befalls the bird is likely to befall you also. Look carefully to see if it takes away a hair from your head with which to build its nest. If it does, then this link between you will be passed along to one of its offspring.

The mountaineers share a belief with the Irish that a raven coming to rest on the rooftop of a home foretells of a death in the household within a fortnight. This prophecy can be thwarted by having something with which to scare away the ravens before they fly off of their own accord. The only catch is that, to accomplish this feat, neither human gestures nor voices can be used. To fall prey to this natural inclination to rush the birds only cuts in half the time left for the doomed one. The usual choices for scaring away the ravens are gunshots or rocks thrown at the roof. Causing a dog to bark or charge the house is also fair play.

If a blackbird comes to rest on a windowsill of your home, it is generally a bad omen, but if it takes anything away with it, or caws at you while sitting there, the ill luck becomes a death in the family. Fortunately, there are two ways to negate this omen. In the case of the bird removing an object from the windowsill you should, of course, follow the bird to its nest and retrieve the object. In the case of the bird coming to caw at your window, only killing the creature after it has started to fly away, then burning it at the edge of the local cemetery will do. This latter is a form of sympathetic magick known as *magickal substitution* in which one item or need is exchanged for a greater one. In this case the death of the bird, and its interment in the graveyard, acts as a magickal replacement for the person who was marked to die. Keep in mind that it pays to know your blackbirds in the mountain. If the bird who comes to your windowsill is a crow, it indicates a possible blight on your land or a famine, and his presence is not considered a death omen.

Owls, those birds of wisdom and knowledge in European folklore, are viewed in Appalachia as being wholly evil. Some even go so far as to say they are in the service of Satan himself. If you encounter an owl in the mountain woods, give it a wide berth, and heed its warning if you feel it is telling you to leave. To thwart its wishes is to ask for curses upon yourself and your land. If an owl is seen flying directly over your home, a death will shortly follow.

A rooster heard crowing at midnight heralds a death within the community. A crowing hen is also a death omen which can be thwarted only by killing her and then wiping her blood on your door post, or by killing and burying her at a crossroad. In old Ireland and Scotland, the crossroad was a natural equal-armed cross, an ancient symbol of defense and balance, and much magick for self-protection is still performed there.

A dog howling three times in succession after dark also heralds a death. To find out who it will be, you need only stand behind the animal and look just over his head between his ears. The face of the victim should be seen suspended there.

Most of the Appalachian range is covered with thick, lush foliage, but there are rocky areas, particularly where strip mining and other abuses to the land have occurred. Being hit by a rock falling off a mountainside without human or animal aid can magickally open a hole in the body through which gorm can escape. The word "gorm" is a southern mountain colloquialism for the human soul or life-force, which may be in some way related to the same British slang term which means "to smear." To remove this curse you must take the rock, along with two others of a similar size and color, to the nearest body of running water. Stand at the water's edge and cast the stones in, one at a time, in the name of the Father, Son, and Holy Ghost. Pagans, Goddess worshippers, and others who follow non-mainstream religions should feel free to substitute the names of any of the Triple Goddesses in this spell.[7] These deities, representing the maiden, mother, and crone aspects of the Goddess, have had their names used in similar spells throughout Europe for many centuries, and this ancient practice is likely at the root of this folk spell.

Allowing a digging tool to be brought into the house is a sign that a grave will need to be dug before the year is out. If it is allowed to rest against an interior wall, it indicates an outbreak of illness in the household which will affect many before one is carried away by death. Breaking the tool in half and burying it in two separate places will break this curse.

Seeing "torch lights" moving through the woods at night is a portent of one's own demise. At one time the folk wisdom of the mountains said these were the spirits of the cemetery on parade to honor the one soon to be in their midst. In truth, what people were probably seeing was a phenomenon known in the mountains as "foxfire." The rest of us know these strange night lights as the elusive will-o'-the-wisp, a luminescence which dances tantalizingly in the distance, but mysteriously moves away when approached.[8] Science has never adequately explained these lights, though some of them have been attributed to gases which are released as organic matter decomposes.[9]

If a clock begins to make a strange noise or run erratically, it is a sign that a death is occurring in the extended family at that very moment. If a clock stops suddenly for no apparent reason, it means the death of the eldest family member. If a clock or watch which has not been functioning suddenly begins working again, it means that it has bound itself to the life of someone in the home and will stop again only at that person's demise.

To dream of riding a black horse is another death omen. Whoever is seen riding the horse is the potential victim. Dreams about muddy water, about crossing over water, about falling out of a tree, or being lost in a cave are other well-known death omens.

Hearing someone laugh in their sleep, whether or not they remember dreaming, is another sign of approaching death.

If you hear the sound of shattering glass when none has been broken, it foretells the death of someone in your acquaintance within a fortnight. If you clearly hear the voice of someone who has died recently, it heralds another death in the family within a year's time.

From old Scotland comes another omen which found a new home in Appalachia: that of seeing one's "fetch." A fetch, sometimes incorrectly referred to as a *doppelgänger*,[10] is an exact duplicate of yourself, only in spectral form, which appears to let you know it has been sent to "fetch you" shortly to the land of the dead. Most often it appears standing behind you as you gaze into some reflective surface. When you turn to look at it, it will vanish from your sight, but if you look back into the reflective surface, you will see that it remains behind you. Death is said to occur within a fortnight of the sighting.

To see a white dog after dark is a very ill omen under any circumstances, but to have it stop and look at you is a portent of your own demise. This is another omen with Scottish roots found in the myths of the *cu sith*, or faery dog of the Highlands.[11] It is possible to turn this omen around if you can take some of the dog's drool and brew it into a tea.[12]

Communal deaths have also been a concern in Appalachia, especially in the decades past when epidemics of typhoid and smallpox were not uncommon.[13] When the snowbush, a white blooming mountain tree, bloomed early and lush it was a sign that many deaths would occur before it bloomed again the next year. On the other hand, if it bloomed late and sparse, no epidemics would ravage the community during that year.

The sound of an unknown woman singing after dark is a sign that death will come to someone in the community before dawn. This may well be a remnant of the Celtic belief in the banshee (*beansidhe* in Gaelic), a feminine faery spirit who keens a ghostly mourning wail on the night before a death.[14]

A divination for discovering how many deaths will occur within a community in a given season involves using a handful of dried beans and a shovel. Take these objects to a nearby graveyard and set the shovel on the ground in front of you, with the rounded side down. At the stroke of midnight, cry out to the guardian of the cemetery with words such as:

> *Guardian of fearful face,*
> *How many will soon take thy place?*

Toss the beans high into the air and let them land where they will. Either a few or many of the beans may land in the bowl of the shovel. When the beans have settled, pick up the shovel and carry it out of the graveyard without spilling any. After you are well away from the cemetery, count how many beans are in the shovel's bowl and you should know how many deaths will occur before the season's change.[15]

Haints!

The colloquial term "haint" is a derivation of the word "haunt," which in southern Appalachia means a "ghost" or "spirit." The popularity of haint tales in the folklore of the mountains attests to the deep belief in their existence and the amount of energy which has been used to detect, avoid, and banish these beings.

Some of the most bone-chilling haint stories I ever heard were told by my Uncle Bob, who keeps a recreational houseboat on the man-made mountain lake known as Lake Cumberland, in Kentucky. After many summers of soaking up the local atmosphere, he has become quite a spinner of Cumberland Mountain tales. His favorite is the story about the old woman who refused to leave her cabin when the large valley was being flooded in order to create the lake. She swore to government officials that she would die before leaving her family home. Thinking to drive her out by force, the government went ahead and began the flooding of the valley, hoping that the feisty lady would see reason and allow herself to be taken out. However, true to her promise of preferring to die rather than leave, the old lady dropped dead just as the water level reached the front door of her cabin. Uncle Bob assured my cousin and I that her angry spirit haunted the mountain just above our anchorage in a narrow cove, ever searching for those who drove her from her home.

Over the past half century, belief in ghosts has fallen into disfavor and is now looked upon as a sign of backwardness or even ignorance.[16] Yet a significant number of mountain folks still take the haint tales to heart and know many of the old magick remedies for getting rid of them. In contrast to Pagan magickal traditions, no known folk magick spell from Appalachia concerns the invoking of spirits, just banishing them.

Allowing yourself to speak the name of the dead three times in succession can evoke the presence of the one mentioned, hence it is never done. The number three has a long history in evocations in Anglo-Celtic magick. Three was the number of times the name of a deity was called upon to invite his or her presence, and three was the number of times many accused witches reported crying out to invoke the Devil.

A little preventive maintenance can go a long way to help keep you and your home from being haunted. If you know approximately when a death is going to occur in your home, you should open the windows wide ahead of time to allow the spirit to fly free. Keeping them closed will only trap the spirit within the walls, leaving it free to haunt you, and also making it angry.

There are several distinct signs that you are in the presence of a ghost. One is coming across a cat which insists on hissing at nothing. The presence of a strange white dog, or a sheet flapping in the wind are others. Cold spots in a room indicate ghostly presences, as do unidentified rappings from within walls or trees.

A clock which suddenly starts to run backward indicates that you will soon be visited by a ghost.

Certain locations are attractive to ghosts and should best be avoided by the timid, particularly after dark. Among these are narrow woodland trails, at the base of dead trees, wherever lightning has struck, near the banks of isolated creeks and rivers, and of course in burial grounds. Not only were these favored spots for spirits to hang out in Celtic folklore, but Native Americans of the Appalachian region also shared these perceptions, each strengthening the other's belief in their own convictions.

To keep ghosts from coming inside your home, hang some dried basil over the threshold, and place a sprig or two in each windowsill and in front of the fireplace. Rue or purslane planted near the house also discourages ghostly visits, and wild horseradish or mustard placed under a pillow will prevent them from giving you nightmares.

Spinning counterclockwise three times before entering your home is said to confuse the pursuing spirits so that they cannot follow you indoors. Chances are good that this magickal act was once done in tandem with the recitation of a little rhyming chant. Such chants, called charms in the vernacular of the mountains, were clearly once very popular, but fell into disuse sometime around the turn of the century and most have been lost to us. If you would like to add a charm to this action, try one of the following. They are not authentic, but will serve the purpose:

1. *Twisting and turning I laugh with glee,*
   No unwelcome haint can follow me.
2. *Spirit following me this day,*
   Turn around and go away.
3. *Round, and round, and round I spin,*
   No haint or shade can come within.

The number three is also prominent in two other anti-ghost spells: rapping three times on your doorpost before entering your home, and rapping three times on your bedpost before falling asleep.

Hanging small bells on the inside of your door which can ring when the door is opened and shut is an ancient and widespread practice to prevent unwanted spectral beings from entering a dwelling at will whenever the door is opened. Many decorative items we see every day were once used to frighten off spirits, although we may not consciously think about their original functions today. Wind chimes, which have their roots in Pagan China, are the best-known such device, and Scandinavian door harps are another. Door harps are made of wood and resemble the head of a mandolin, with four wire strings strung across the acoustical opening. Above these are suspended four wooden balls which bounce against the strings when the door is opened or closed, making a lovely musical chord. Over the past century, door harps have become quite popular in Appalachia as decorative items. Today, mountain craftspersons hand-make them for sale to the public. Many of them—by design, custom, or coincidence—are carved with magickal or protective symbols.

If you are unsure of the identity of the ghost who is haunting you, take a mirror and a candle, and head for your friendly neighborhood graveyard, preferably timing your sojourn so that you will be there by the stroke of midnight. Lean the mirror up against either the wall of the cemetery or the trunk of a nearby tree. Stand with your back to the mirror and light your candle. Hold the candle out in front of you and stare into the flame for as long as is comfortable (three to five minutes is sufficient). Try to make your mind a blank except for the question of wanting to know the identity of the ghost. When you are done, chant something like:

> *Flame which is the truth of light,*
> *Reveal the face who haunts the night.*

Blow out the candle and turn around quickly to look into the mirror. The face of the spirit should be reflected there.

If you fear your house is already being haunted, one popular remedy says that if you rebuild part of it with fresh-cut timber, the spirit will go away.

If you have done everything you know how to do to protect yourself, but still find yourself face to face with a ghost, you should first turn and walk away from it. However, do not look back under any circumstances, or legend says that you will be the next to die.

There are several magickal ways to banish ghosts from your home or land, the most interesting being to feed the ghost potatoes. Do this by setting out a plate for the restless spirit just after sundown. You may even want to speak aloud and let the ghost know you are leaving a snack just for him. Because of their association with the magical element of earth, potatoes have long been used in grounding rituals, meaning that they channel energy back into the earth and, in this case, may symbolically function as a catalyst to return the wandering spirit to its grave. Bury the potatoes at dawn and your ghost should be buried with them.

Death, Dying, and "Haints"

From the North Carolina Blue Ridge comes another potato exorcism which can be used if you know the identity of your restless spirit. Take an unwashed, unpeeled potato and cut it in half. Then, with a knife or grapefruit spoon, hollow out a small section of the center, being careful not to cut out so much meat that the walls are weakened. Take a small, non-valued item which once belonged to the deceased and place it inside this hole. With two long nails or pins, reseal the potato and bury it as near to the ghost's grave as you can. This should keep the haint bound within the confines of the cemetery until it is ready to move on.

Gunshots fired to the four cardinal directions (west, north, east, and south) from each corner of your house will also frighten away any ghosts or evil spirits lurking nearby. Chanting "ghost be gone" three times upon waking and upon going to bed, three days in succession, is also reputed to work. Or you could resort to tossing vile-smelling herbs on the hearth which will not only drive out ghosts, but probably anyone else with whom you live.

Mountain Monsters and Faeries

Though less well-known than the Pacific Northwest's Bigfoot or Scotland's Loch Ness Monster, the woods and lakes of southern Appalachia are reputed to have their own mysterious inhabitants who keep their own legends alive by making an appearance every fifty years or so.

One of the most famous lake monsters is a creature sometimes referred to as "Miss Tallulah," who was first sighted by several people near Tallulah Falls in Georgia in 1892. The creature is described as being scaly and serpentine, similar to the reported appearance of the Loch Ness Monster, but decidedly smaller in length. Several sightings of Miss Tallulah have been reported over the last century, and every one was within one year prior to some event of major world importance. The 1892 sighting came just before the economic panic of 1893, and other sightings were reported prior to the bombing of Pearl Harbor in 1941 and the assassination of President John Kennedy in 1963.

Ever since human beings first came to the mountains there have been occasional reports of huge ape-man type creatures roaming in the dense backwoods. These are similar to the reported sightings of Bigfoot (also called Sasquatch or the Yeti) in other parts of the world. These sightings always occur in remote forested areas, and the creatures invariably flee when they realize that they are being observed by humans. In keeping with the lore of these creatures from other places in the world, no one has ever been known to be harmed by one of them.

The Scots brought to the mountains with them some of their faery lore. Belief in house sprites who can help or harm was once quite prevalent; however beliefs about the specific nature of faeries seems to have died out over the last few decades, leaving behind only a vagueness about who and what these creatures represent. Mountaineers still refer to meadows covered with the herb meadowsweet as "faery meadows," places where one can lose all track of time, time being irrelevant in the faery world. It was considered very dangerous to allow one's self to be lured to sleep here since the enchanted meadowsweet would produce a "death sleep" from which it was very hard to awaken. If you do wish to nap in one of the faery meadows, first take the precaution of placing some iron in your pockets, a metal which will render faeries powerless over you.

The inhabitants of these meadows may be the Cherokee faeries known as the Nunnehi (pronounced Nun-AY-hee) who were made known to the mountain folk in the early nineteenth century. The Nunnehi are burgh-dwelling sprites who were friends and allies of the Cherokee, perhaps even their ancestor spirits. They were credited with assisting the lost to find their way back to their tribes and were even said to take up arms against their common enemies. When the Cherokee were banished westward along the Trail of Tears, the Nunnehi's own tears of sorrow became the dark crystalline stone of the area, which sometimes appears in the shape of an equilateral cross. These are prized talismans of protection in the mountains.

Another woodland creature is called the jackro, whose name may come from the Irish slang term "jackaroo" which refers to an irresponsible or roguish man. As one would expect, a jackro is a mischievous creature who likes to play tricks on people he finds wandering in the forest. He's not a bad fellow, just annoying. You can protect yourself against his pranks by carrying a protective talisman or amulet with you as you travel the mountain trails.

Magickal Self-Protection

Many of the protection rites found in Appalachia have clear roots in the pre-Christian magickal beliefs of western Europe. For instance, in Appalachia, wearing a metal object on the left thigh was once a common protection to prevent spells being cast upon the wearer by witches. This can be traced to a similar Scottish practice which used a brooch for the same purpose.

If you feel you are being followed by an evil spirit, you should cross over running water. The spirit's power will be grounded since it cannot pass over the stream.

If you are being followed by a suspected witch, stop in your tracks, turn counterclockwise three times, and spit on the road. You may then continue on, confident that the witch cannot take his or her power past the spot where you expectorated.

Tossing nine broom straws, one at a time, on a hearth fire at sunset will turn away predators of human, spectral, or animal nature.

Animal skins hung on the wall of a home will help ward off unwanted specters, and most mountain cabins had—and some still have—several pelts hanging around.

If you fear someone is going to put a curse on you, tie up a lock of your hair, a stick from your yard, and a clipped nail with a red string, and carry it in your pocket. As long as this is in your possession you cannot be cursed. However, if you lose the talisman, there is a chance it could be found by an enemy who will use it against you.

Having a "witch peg" in the house is the best preventative against curses sent your way. A witch peg is a three pronged spike cut from cedar wood which is kept near the front door or under a bed. It can be driven into the side of your home or the ground if need be to channel evil into the earth away from you. You can also wipe blood on the peg first to double the protective power.

By the late medieval period, Halloween, the descendant of the old Celtic Pagan festival of Samhain, had been diabolized to hellish proportions. On this night, when Pagans see the world of spirit and matter as being comfortably close, the mountain folk, true to their medieval heritage, see the night as an evil thing, and will usually elect to stay indoors for the sake of their own souls. On this night, and on others where spirits are thought to be running free (such as after a funeral or when it is storming), staying indoors is the most often prescribed remedy.

Endnotes to Chapter 2

1. The death obsession can be noted in most of the books in the Bibliography which deal with the social conventions or folklife of the mountains.
2. Baker, Margaret. *Folklore and Customs of Rural England* (Totowa, NJ: Rowman and Littlefield, Co., 1974).
3. Wigginton, Eliot, ed. *The Foxfire Book* (Garden City, NY: Doubleday and Co., 1972) p. 306.
4. McCoy, Edain. *A Witch's Guide to Faery Folk* (St. Paul, MN: Llewellyn Worldwide, 1994) pp. 64–67.
5. Baker, p. 92.

6. For example, the myth of Blodeuwedd who was transformed into an owl. For further discussion, please see my earlier work, *Celtic Myth and Magick* (Llewellyn, 1995).

7. For a full discussion see D. J. Conway's *Maiden, Mother and Crone: The Myth and Reality of the Triple Goddess* (Llewellyn, 1994).

8. McCoy, p. 338.

9. See the Introduction to *Foxfire 9* for a discussion of the scientific point of view. Reynolds, George P. and students, eds. (New York: Doubleday and Co., 1986).

10. A doppelgänger is defined as an exact duplicate of a person, which can be seem by others just beside the physical body, simultaneously performing the same task or action as the body. The fetch appears to be a different sort of spirit, one which is otherworldly in origin, whose sole function seems to be to warn a person of their own impending death. For further discussion, and to read recorded cases of doppelgänger and fetch sightings (primarily from Europe), please refer to John and Anne Spencer's *The Encyclopedia of Ghosts and Spirits* (London: Headline Books, 1992).

11. McCoy, p. 185.

12. This is not a recommended practice, since it is also a good way to give yourself rabies. If you want a magickal way to overcome this omen, I suggest looking through other texts on magickal protection for an alternate method which appeals to you.

13. Dargan, Olive T. *Highland Annals* (New York: Scribner & Sons, 1925). Several excellent fiction-based-on-fact accounts can also be located.

14. McCoy, pp. 181-183.

15. For an example of adapting this spell to the beliefs of another magickal tradition, please see Chapter 8.

16. Reynolds, *Foxfire 9*.

CHAPTER THREE

The Magick of Health and Healing

I love my love and well he knows,
I love the ground on where he goes,
If he on earth no more I could see,
My life would quickly fade from me.
    —Traditional Mountain Air

Two hundred years of isolation from standard medical care partially explains the deeply ingrained distrust of doctors which has often been attributed to the people of Appalachia. For almost two centuries they relied solely on their witches and granny women to provide folk magick and folk medicine to heal them of their ills. Over the course of the twentieth century, faith healing, a fundamentalist Christian belief in absolution from sickness by reliance upon their God, has gained in popularity and further undermined conventional medicine. There is also a strong native belief—one with Jewish roots—which has often been heard quoted in the mountains: that God did not put any illness on the planet for which he did not also provide the cure. It is just up to us to find that cure. Put all these factors together and you get a picture of a people who believe in taking care of their own by using the old familiar ways, ones which have been passed down to them over many generations.

Most of the cures from the southern mountains consist of an intriguing combination of folk magick and folk medicine. Folk medicine differs from magickal healing in that the actions taken to effect the cure are designed to have a direct, medicinal impact on the illness. For example, hanging herbs around your neck to drive out tuberculosis is folk magick, drinking an herbal concoction containing natural expectorants is folk medicine.

Herbalism, the knowledge of and use of vegetation for either magick or medicine, is the mainstay of Appalachian healers. As in Europe, many of the common mountain plants are known by a variety of colorful folk names which often provide glimpses into the appearance, uses, or associations of a particular piece of foliage. For instance, wild ginger's more common name is "monkey jugs," called so to describe their little jug-shaped leaves, and boneset is sometimes called "up-and-about," indicating its medicinal use as a fever reducer and fracture mender.

Using botanical nicknames when copying a spell into a magickal diary is not only fun, but it is a time-honored practice, one whose original intent was likely secrecy. The following is a list of some of the more popular nicknames for Appalachian herbs, trees, and wildflowers[1]:

Common Name	Folk Name(s)
Asafetida	Devil's Dung
Basil	Witch Wort
Belladonna	Nightshade, Lych Weed
Black Cohosh	Indian Pipe, Black Snake Root
Blackberry	Bramble, Dewberry
Boneset	Up-and-about
Buckeye	Horse Chestnut
Calmus	Moonroot

Common Name	Folk Name(s)
Celedine	Kenning Wort
Chickweed	Winterweed
Comfrey	Feverfew, Knitbone, Augeweed
Cowslip	Faery Cups
Crabapple	Robber Weed
Dandelion	Swine Snout, Buttercup
Elder	Faery Tree, Black Box
Foxglove	Heart Start, Faery Wort
Galax	Turtlehead
Garlic	Stink Weed
Hops	Ale Wort, Indian Slap
Horseradish	Head Pops
Lily of the Valley	Dead Man's Bells
Linden	Lime Tree
Lippia	Hawk Weed
Lobelia	Pukeweed, Witch Pod
Mayflower	Cunning Wort
Meadow Onion	Mallow Weed
Meadowsweet	Faery Trumpet, Bridewort
Mustard	Devil's Fly
Myrtle	Matchmaker
Pennyroyal	Meadow Mint
Plantain	Snake Weed
Pokeberry	Inkberry
Purslane	Pigweed
Raspberry	Flux Wort
Red Clover	Strong Man
Rhododendron	Passion Petes
Rosemary	Bane-be-gone, Love Myrtle
Rue	Faery Flute
Slippery Elm	Indian Balm
Strawberry Shrub	Bubby Blossoms
Trillium	Ground Ivy, Trinity Weed
Valerian Root	Graveyard Dust, Catnip
Violet, Purple	Sweet Mary, Farsight
Violet, Giant	Crow's Feet, Birdsfoot
Violet, White	Virgin Flower
Wild Ginger	Monkey Jugs
Woodruff	Sweet Willie
Yarrow	Arrowroot, Savior Plant

A Word of Warning to the Wise

The best way to use folk magick and/or medicine in healing is to employ them in tandem with modern medicine. More than ever, today's doctors and other health-care practitioners are recognizing the wisdom inherent in many of the old remedies, and are willing to assist their patients in the use of them. Never, under any circumstances, should someone who needs to see a doctor rely solely on magick to affect a cure. Magick just does not work that way. It expects you to do as much as you can in the physical world to aid yourself, and if this means seeing a doctor, then you should do so immediately.

The Appalachian folk are masters at effectively using highly toxic herbs to work many of their cures. Some of these plants have been studied to find the cause of their power, and from them many life-saving modern medicines, such as digitalis (a heart medication) from foxglove, have been derived. However, layfolk, those not professionally involved in the healing arts, *should not try to duplicate the use of these poisonous herbs*. Many have tried and died for their efforts. Aside from poisonous substances, there are numerous mountain healing spells and folk medicines which contain feces, urine, and other unhealthful substances which are *not recommended* for use. Several of these spells and cures are included here because they are traditional and make up a large part of the popular healing magick of Appalachia, and I feel that to leave these out would diminish the value of this chapter. Again, healing recipes which call for toxic or dangerous sybstances should be viewed as education material *only*, and should not be put to use.

Neither author nor publisher in any way advocates the use of toxic herbs and other potentially harmful substances for either magick or medicine, and neither the author nor publisher can assume any responsibility for the side effects of experimentation with them. To make these cures easier to spot as you read, an asterisk (*) appears after the name of each poisonous or unhealthful ingredient.

Even when using non-toxic substances in your folk medicine, caution and common sense should guide your hand. Unless you are well-schooled enough in pharmacology to understand the long-term effects of any herb you are taking, it is best to avoid lengthy exposure. For example, I had a friend who was taking eyebright to help strengthen her vision after prescription kidney medicine had caused some temporary damage. Eyebright is generally considered to be harmless, and can be found in teas and capsules in most health food stores. Quite by chance she mentioned her self-treatment to her brother, a professional botanist. He warned her that a certain chemical in eyebright is known to cause the kind of ocular pressure which can lead to glaucoma.

Other unpleasant, or even deadly, side effects can result from allergic reactions. What may be an innocuous substance to another person may be life threatening with your body chemistry. Test any never-before-tried herb or plant twice before using it as a medicine, by administering minute amounts at twenty-four hour intervals. If after the second application you see no redness or swelling, have no signs of itching or hives, no runny nose or tight throat, then you can probably assume that the substance is safe for you to use at this time. Be aware that allergies can come and go throughout life, and if you are normally sensitive to ingested substances you should re-test yourself before each round of treatment.

If you are not an expert on plant identification DO NOT attempt to medicate yourself with plants you have picked in the wild, even if they look exactly like the picture you have of what you need. This is only common sense. Many wild herbs look alike and can be easily mistaken for one another. The best way to get your herbs is from a health food store or by mail order (see Appendix A for addresses). If you want to grow your own herbs, many of the herbal mail order companies will be glad to send you seeds or seedlings with instructions on how best to cultivate them.

Once again, please—please—be cautious when planning any magickal or natural healing regime.

Tonics and Preventive Medicine and Magick

Long after the discovery of antibiotics and proper sanitation made widespread outbreaks of tuberculosis, trachoma, and typhoid (called the "brown death" in the mountains) virtually unheard of elsewhere in the United States, epidemics were regularly rampaging through mountain communities. Many of these illnesses progressed into rapidly advancing forms of pneumonia which killed quickly. The best weapon many mountaineers felt they had against these dread diseases was preventive medicine, which often took the form of tonics.

Spring was the favored time to begin administering these homemade tonics, due to a belief that winter naturally weakened a body, and that it was dangerous to go into the warmer seasons, when conditions were ripe for epidemics, without first strengthening the body's natural immunities.

A favorite spring tonic is made from sassafras blossoms and sourwood honey, from sourwood or hollow black gum trees. Sourwood honey has made Appalachia famous and the unique taste is sought after by connoisseurs and gourmets the world over.[2] Sourwood honey is also combined with sulphur and molasses for medicating families year-round. Sulphur is easy to come by due to the numerous sulphur springs and creeks which run through the hills.

Collecting and boiling rust for drinking is another favorite tonic. Though the healthfulness of this practice is questionable, there is little doubt that the iron content did appear to provide amazing results in a region where sufficient iron in the diet is lacking. Another iron-rich tonic is a tea made from a combination of red clover and blue cohosh root, one often given to new mothers to reduce the risk of childbed fever.

In Carroll and Grayson counties in southwestern Virginia, pumpkin seeds are sometimes set to roasting in homes as a way to prevent winter ailments, or to ward off local epidemics. Each fall, dry the seeds and then seal them in a clean glass jar to have a supply on hand for the coming year.

Meadow onion, a garlic-like plant which shares garlic's antibiotic property *alliin*, is another preventive tonic of great repute, and the herb is often used to season many mountain dishes. It has even been placed under pillows, though this is not recommended unless you enjoy dreaming about food.

A magickal way to protect health is to take a bean and slice it in half. Prick a finger from your right hand and put a drop of blood into the bean. Press the bean back together and plant it near your home. Repeat as often as needed.

Alzheimer's Disease

Known in the past as senility or old age dementia, Alzheimer's is characterized by mental confusion and loss of recent memory. Drinking cowslip tea is reputed to help the forgetfulness, or you could simply opt for sleeping with a dirty diaper(*).

Arthritis

Over 100 different arthritic illnesses have been classified by the American Arthritis Foundation, but perhaps none has been more the focus of folk healing in both North American and Europe as rheumatoid arthritis, commonly called rheumatism.

Make a poultice of warm ginseng which has been placed between two sheets of white linen. Apply this to the affected joints overnight for relief.

Carry a buckeye in your left pocket to ease joint pain. Change the old buckeye for a new one when the joints stop aching to prevent new inflammation.

Roasted pokeberry roots(*) can be applied to the joints, but are said to draw out the pain best if they are used after dark.

If a tornado hits your home, anyone under its roof who has arthritis will be immediately and permanently cured.

You can attempt to scare yourself out of pain by having a willing helper come up with some creative surprises.

Bees have much magickal significance in Appalachia, and their venom, either applied to the joints or placed in a tea, is reputed to work wonders for severe rheumatic distress. (Good cure or not, if you are known to be allergic to bee stings, DO NOT use the venom in any way!)

Wearing copper is an old arthritis cure found on many continents, as are daily doses of alfalfa leaf teas. Both of these remedies are also known in Appalachia.

Home-brewed whiskey, known popularly as moonshine or white mule, is another popular cure for arthritis. Those who were fans of the 1960s sitcom, "The Beverly Hillbillies," will no doubt remember Granny Clampitt working over her still (a copper-pipe contraption which distills whiskey), brewing up a batch of her "roomatiz medicine."[3]

You might also try relieving the pain by pricking the affected joint with a pin, then taking the pin to the nearest graveyard and pushing it deep into the ground.

Asthma

Asthma is caused by a severe, contracting spasm of the bronchial tubes, brought on either by allergic reactions or by emotional duress.

Eating radishes dipped in sourwood honey will help ease breathing during an attack, as will a cup of extra-strong coffee. Eating dried wild horseradish, wild mustard, or an herb known as lippia, which grows wild in the foothills of the mountains, will help open the bronchial tubes and relax the chest muscles. Lippia is also an excellent expectorant.

A magickal measure for preventing asthma says to cut off a lock of your hair and seal it up in a sourwood tree. In a week's time, return to the tree and make it an offering of bread. Leave the offering at the tree's base overnight. If the bread is gone the next morning, the tree has accepted your offering and will absorb your asthma from the hair left inside it.

Backaches

A popular preventative remedy for backaches says that when you hear the first bird of spring call to you, you should turn three quick somersaults. This will protect you for the coming year as long as you didn't hurt yourself making the heels-over-head flips in the first place.

To magickally cure persistent backaches, take off all your clothes from the waist up, and have someone take "graveyard dust" (a name for ground valerian root) and rub a thin layer all over your back. Then, without dressing, stand on your head for a count of one hundred. Wash off the herb dust with a cloth dampened with whiskey.

Old-timers insist that sleeping regularly on a horsehair mattress will rend the sleeper impervious to back trouble.

Bites and Stings

A damp mixture of nettles (*), tobacco juice(*), or ragweed will take out the sting of insect bites or bee stings.

Boiled oak leaves applied to spider bites will take out the itch and reduce swelling as long as the bite is not from a poisonous spider.

Wearing plantain while walking or working in the woods, or carrying a white stone from a graveyard, will prevent snakebite. Or you can spit on the first dead log you come across on your trek and know you are protected.

Black Lung

Black lung is a disease found among coal miners in which the lungs become coated with a fine layer of coal dust inhaled while working in the mines. The condition often mimics the symptoms of lung cancer or tuberculosis, and is nearly impossible to cure even with modern medicine. However, the symptoms can be treated with hospitalization.

The mountain folk believe that eating apples every day can restore the lungs to their normal condition, as long as the miner also gives up his occupation.

Chewing calmus(*) root while working in the mine is also thought to help protect the lungs.

Bladder Infections

The burning pain of bladder and urinary tract infections is another condition to which folk healing devotes much lore. Some methods of curing it are more effective than others.

Drinking liquid of any kind to flush out the microbes causing the infection is always the best remedy, but if you can find a substance particularly useful in killing the microbes and helping to prevent reinfection, all the better. Teas made from nettles(*), cowslip, or dandelions are all effective against the cause of the infection. Each of these contains vitamin C, which has been shown to produce an environment in the bladder hostile to the microbes.

Making a cake using your own urine(*) and then eating it is another trick for affecting a cure.

A magical solution is to take a cupful of urine(*) out to a birch tree and pour it around the roots while walking three times counterclockwise. Pull off a small piece of bark to take with you, then return home without looking back. Carry the bark with you until cured, then bury it back at the base of the tree.

Burns

One of the best remedies for burns was passed along to the mountain folk from the Cherokee. Blend equal parts crushed slippery elm bark and cornmeal. Add enough water to make a thick paste and apply. This aids the healing process and will take out the sting.

Another effective burn paste can be made from egg whites, baking soda, and linseed oil.

Many other salves popular in the mountains contain less than appealing ingredients. Nasal mucus(*) is one such remedy, as is a poultice made from cow feces(*) and lard.

To keep a burn from leaving a scar, take a stone from your own yard and, with fireproof tongs, hold it in the fireplace (a candle flame will do) until it is literally red hot. As it heats, picture the stone removing the burn from your skin, taking the burn into itself. Being careful not to burn yourself again on the hot stone, take it outdoors and bury it, or drop it in a cool lake or river.

Chapped Skin

Rubbing your hands with the first snow of the season is supposed to keep your hands from chapping all winter long. If this fails, a salve for chapped skin can be made from lard, birch leaves, and pine resin.

Children and Infants

Cure bedwetting by taking a drop of the child's blood(*) and dropping it onto a grain which you feed to a black hen. Or you can administer a spoonful of elderberry wine at bedtime which has been stirred with a black hen's tail feather.

Colic can be cured with a regular dose of stillingia root juice, ginseng root, or kerosene(*).

Stomach distress can be eased with a plantain poultice.

Making talismans for the baby's room from swine's teeth will help a baby through the trials of teething.

Colds, Flu, and Congestion

In Appalachia, it is said that eating spider webs on moldy bread will help draw out the infection of a cold or flu.

A poultice of gently warmed onions and lard is good for chest congestion. Turpentine(*) and lard is another popular chest poultice.

Red clover tea will help dry up a runny nose.

White cedar leaves, white pine bark, senega (known as mountain flax), coltsfoot, lippia, and juniper berries(*) are all much-used expectorants, which will help break up chest congestion.

A few drops of distilled pleurisy root in hot water will help break up a chest cold.

To ease the cough of a cold or flu, mix up a brew of mullein roots, sugar, honey, and wild cherry bark.

Spitting at the waning moon while cursing the Devil is thought to help speed the cure and prevent the cold from running into pneumonia.

Red pepper tea is an excellent nasal decongestant, but if this fails, and you have congestion which just will not go away, take yourself to the graveyard and roll on top of an old enemy's grave. The congestion should break up within the next three days.

Contraception

Mountain women who drink a tea during their fertile periods made from the seeds of the flowering herb called Queen Anne's Lace report it to be an excellent contraceptive.

Like many grains, corn is an ancient symbol of fertility, so to symbolically destroy it would be an act of sympathetic magick designed to prevent pregnancy. Mountain women have been known to burn or blacken corn ears or cobs and place them either under their beds or the front porch. If the corn was discolored to begin with—even better!

Cramps of All Types

To prevent leg and foot cramps from waking you in the night, turn your shoes upside down before going to bed. You should also get into bed by going "feet first." This is best accomplished by stepping up onto the mattress as if it were part of a steep staircase rather than trying to crawl in upside down.

Tie a red string around the handle (called the "dash") of a butterchurn before going to bed to prevent charley-horses.

Diets rich in garlic and other heavy spices are also supposed to help ward off night leg cramps.

Menstrual cramps can be treated with a soothing wild raspberry tea to which a little moonshine and sourwood honey has been added. Or they can be avoided altogether by making an offering of beets outside of a graveyard the day after your period has ended.

Burying crabapples and jack-in-the-pulpits near your outhouse (in the absence of an outhouse, try burying these over wherever you think your plumbing pipes might run) will stop cramps and will help prevent miscarriages as well.

Constipation

Take a spoonful of lard and turpentine(*) each hour until cured, or eat lots of ripe, raw persimmons!

Cuts and Lacerations

Spider webs placed over open cuts will stop them from bleeding. In the absence of an available web, try lamp black(*) or chimney soot(*).

Pine resin will help stop the bleeding as well as disinfect and help in healing.

A walnut poultice is also a good disinfectant. Try mixing this in a paste with a few warm onions for best results.

Dandruff

Wash away those annoying white flakes with an after-shampoo rinse of hops and sage.

Diarrhea

More than any other aspect of sickness, diarrhea will keep us bound to our homes, and feeling drained of energy. Probably nothing makes an illness more miserable.

Teas useful in combating diarrhea include those made of thyme, red oak bark, persimmon bark, and chimney soot(*). Eating blackberries is also helpful.

Drunkenness

Eating cucumbers dipped in a mixture of honey and vinegar not only eases the pains of drunkenness, but also helps purify the blood and strengthen the person.

Earaches

Having someone blow tobacco smoke in an aching ear is a trick learned from Native Americans which many folks, both in and out of the mountains, swear by. Or you can have the affected person hold their head near a fire or open flame in an effort to burn out the pain.

With an eyedropper, put two or three drops of any of the following in your ear: sweet shrub juice (called "buddy blooms" in Appalachia), lukewarm saltwater with a bit of rubbing alcohol, juice from cooked cabbage, the blood of a black spider(*), or urine(*).

For a magickal cure, tie galax leaves around your head and wear them overnight. The next morning, bury them near a creek.

Or try standing on your head to the count of 100, while a dog licks your face.

Edema

Edema is the retention of water in the legs, which causes uncomfortable swelling. The most often-used mountain remedy is a comfrey and clover poultice.

Elevating your legs and cutting down on salt consumption are also useful treatments.

Some swear they find relief only by soaking their feet or legs in natural sulphur springs.

Epilepsy and "Fits"

To prevent epileptic seizures, mountain wisdom says that you should first cut a large round hole in a tree, retaining the plug for later use. First thing the next morning, shave your head and take the hair to the tree and place it inside the hole. Using the plug, seal the hair in the tree with a charm such as:

> *From my head the fits are shorn,*
> *A cure I make on this fine morn.*

Tea made from lobelia(*), a plant containing anti-spasmodic alkaloids, can help keep seizures to a minimum.

Having a person who is prone to fits run naked through a cemetery in winter is another well-known cure.

Fevers

Fever is one of the body's first signs that something is wrong. Since there are few illnesses which do not produce fever as a symptom, it is not surprising that numerous recipes and magickal cures for fever reducers are known the world over. The most popular medicinal preparations used in Appalachia are found in teas made from the following plants, either alone or in combination with each other: linden flowers, willow bark, boneset, comfrey, wild ginger, or pennyroyal leaves(*).

There are also numerous magickal cures for fevers. The most popular is taking nail clippings from the ill person, wrapping them in yellow poplar leaves (commonly called the tulip tree), and taking them to a river to an eel who will carry them away. With the nail clippings will go the fever.

Nail clippings can also be taken to the mouth of a cave and left there in the hope that the spirits of the cave will take them in and, when they do, the fever will disappear.

Hair clippings cut from the head of the sick person should be packed in ice, wrapped in a white cloth, and taken out to an isolated place. Walk around in solitude until you hear a tree mentally call to you, offering its assistance. Place the bundle securely in the branches of the tree and walk away. As long as the bundle does not become dislodged, the fever should start to break as soon as the ice has completely melted.

Sleep all night in an oak tree to break a fever, or sleep with an acorn under your back.

Wearing blue, or being covered in a blue blanket, will also help reduce the fever. Anoint the blanket lightly with vinegar water first for best results.

In Pagan Europe, doorways and thresholds had deep magickal significance, representing change and creating a portal between different worlds of existence. Perhaps it is that symbolism which is at work in the following cure: Have the sick person stand inside a doorway and press his or her arms hard against the doorjamb while reciting a charm such as:

> *Here I stand in no man's land, neither out*
> *nor in.*
> *Burning fire the way is clear, follow not*
> *within.*

The person should return to bed and wait for the fever to break.

For a divination to determine if the person in question will recover from the fever, take some of his or her nail clippings to the cemetery at sunset and bury them. Mark the site with three smooth stones and walk away without looking back. Return at sunrise and, if the stones have not been disturbed, the person will get well.

Fractures

A very widespread mountain belief is that if you slather the area of a broken bone with some of the red clay native to the region, and allow it to dry thoroughly before being washed off prior to setting the bone, that the break will mend fast and straight.

As its name indicates, boneset tea is also useful to help heal the bones, but is toxic in large or repeated doses.

Gout

Gout is a painful inflammation of the joints, usually in the lower legs and feet, caused by poor metabolism of uric acid proteins. While gout is more uncomfortable than it is dangerous, prolonged or frequent attacks can damage bones.

Taking a young dog to bed will cure the gout. The cure will be most efficacious if the dog is yellow.

A treatment for the pain is to eat saffron roots, herbs which are naturally shaped like gout-ridden feet. The roots have been found to contain a natural painkiller called colchicine.

To help the body process the acids which cause gout, you can try drinking large quantities of an acidic liquid such as cranberry juice or vinegar water.

One popular spell for preventing future attacks of gout says you must take either huckleberry or pigweed and, at sundown, rub it over the area most often affected. At midnight take the herbs to the graveyard and, with your right big toe, push them into the soft earth. The herbs must be completely covered for the spell to work, and you must not use your hands to dig.

Hair Loss

When you begin losing your hair, toss a couple of egg whites into your own urine(*) and use this as a shampoo.

Rosemary also makes a good hair wash, since it helps clean oils out from near the hair roots which can contribute to hair loss.

In keeping with the old magickal adage of keeping silent about one's magick, granny women say you should never tell anyone that you are losing your hair or are attempting to treat it for fear of having them make the condition worse.

Headaches

A cool vinegar compress is the most widely known mountain remedy for headaches. Less common, but said to be equally effective, is a poultice made from horseradish leaves.

Some folk swear by sticking your head in an empty flour sack while counting to 100.

Pine needles are sometimes employed and stuck into the scalp like acupuncture needles. Granny women are reputed to be highly skilled at this art.

Inhaling a potpourri of linden flowers, rhododendron(*), wild violets, and cloves might also be tried.

For persistent or debilitating headaches, the victim who shuns medical help might turn to mountain magick. Taking one's hair clippings and burying them under a large rock will keep headaches at bay as long as the stone is not disturbed.

Wearing a metal pan on your head overnight has been tried as a headache cure, and so has tying a yellow or green string around the head. In the morning remove the string and burn it.

Another spell involves taking laurel leaves(*) and placing them in every window of your house, while singing a song to praise your God (any deity, male or female, will do). Then spin around three times and knock your head against the wall. Your headache will disappear, or you'll knock yourself senseless, so it won't matter!

Burning clippings from your eyebrows in a candle flame just before dawn is another old bit of magick for preventing headaches.

Heart Problems

NEVER try to treat a heart problem without the advice of a qualified physician or cardiologist. The risks are just too great. Some of the cardioactive herbs used in the mountains can overstimulate the heart, a side effect which could prove dangerous in some conditions. Others can slow the beat too far or even, in larger doses, produce life-threatening arrhythmias.

Foxglove(*) is often made into a strong tea which is used to strengthen a weak heart. It is from this deadly plant that the miracle heart drug digitalis is distilled.

Eating daily doses of ramps and garlic, or drinking lots of dandelion tea, are other tried and true methods for bolstering an ailing heart.

Hepatitis/Jaundice

This liver virus has several forms, one highly contagious. The two most prominent symptoms are a tender abdomen and the yellowing of the whites of the eyes. Bed rest is essential, as is isolation from others to whom the disease might be passed. Since no standardized treatments for the disease have ever been set, most of the mountain remedies work about as well as anything else.

Barberry root, a plant native to Europe which was brought to North America in the seventeenth century, can be made into a tincture and given sparingly, several times a day. This helps reduce the abdominal tenderness and bleaches out the yellow of the jaundice.

If you live with someone with hepatitis, you can magickally protect yourself by washing your hands and face three times a day in a plantain brew. In this case, the magick has merit, since it has been found to contain antiseptic properties.

High Blood Pressure

High blood pressure is another condition which you should not attempt to treat on your own. Allowing it to go unchecked could lead to heart attacks or strokes.

A diet heavy in garlic and onions has long been a folk remedy for keeping blood pressure down, and in recent years medical science has conceded that this does indeed seem to help a great number of people. Sarsaparilla tea is also used in Appalachia to lower blood pressure.

Infertility/Irregular Periods

Mountain women who are having trouble conceiving, or who do not bleed regularly, often try drinking teas made from either bark of the black haw tree, black cohosh root, or couch grass root. (See Chapter Seven for an in-depth discussion of fertility magick and omens.)

Insomnia

There is probably nothing quite so frustrating as lying in bed, unable to sleep. In the middle part of this century, sleeping drugs became fashionable treatments, but were found to have too many side-effects, including addiction, and people began looking to the old folk ways again for more gentle ways to cope with the condition.

Fortunately for most of us, insomnia is only an occasional problem, one which can be treated as needed with natural relaxants. Soothing teas made of catnip, calamus(*), chamomile, valerian root, or houndstongue work wonders, and will not leave you feeling drugged or sluggish in the morning.

For those who suffer acute insomnia, there are magickal remedies. The best known is to spend one night in the graveyard, making sure you are laid out in the same direction as the bodies (which usually face east in the mountains). Do this every Sunday night and you should sleep very soundly the rest of the week, possibly due to the fact that you were too scared to even close your eyes the night before. Exhaustion can work wonders for insomnia.

Bark from either a birch, black locust(*), or elder tree which has been soaked in pig urine(*) and placed under the mattress is also said to be a sound cure. Those prone to nightmares should forgo elder as it is believed to provoke spirits who delight in giving humans bad dreams.

Drinking milk from an eggshell, or turning your covers upside down, or sleeping with your head at the foot of the bed, may also affect a cure.

Lameness

In Appalachia, lameness is an all-inclusive label applied to any condition which prevents a person from walking properly, be it from a sprain, injury, or birth defect. Kissing a mule on the mouth is the most common magickal cure.

Malaria

Characterized by intermittent fevers and chills, malaria is transmitted by mosquitoes carrying a tiny protozoa. Fortunately, this disease has been virtually eliminated from Europe and North America.

However, if you are traveling to an area where contact with malaria is likely, protect yourself by catching a toad at dawn and blowing your breath into its mouth. Then set it down and allow it go on its way unharmed. As long as it lives, it will keep the malaria from you.

Wearing a spider(*) in a pouch over your left thigh is another remedy.

Nosebleed

To stop a persistent nosebleed, try hanging pot hooks about your neck, or lying down on an ancestor's grave at dusk and dawn.

A compress of myrtle and birch bark will help constrict the blood vessels and stop the bleeding.

In the Blue Ridge, some rural folk keep wooden pegs handy in the medicine cabinet. Wipe the blood from your nose on the peg and hammer it into a tree. The nosebleed should stop as soon as this is done.

Poison Ivy/Itching

This trifoliate plant has been the bane of campers and woodsfolk for a long time and, since only two percent of the North American population is immune to the itching and blistering caused by contact with it, there are several remedies.

A wash of buttermilk and vinegar will help to stop itching, as will a paste made from baking soda, wild touch-me-not, and hops.

To speed healing, cover the affected areas with red clay and allow them to dry.

Carrying trillium, a plentiful mountain wildflower, in your pocket when out in infested areas is supposed to help prevent infection in the first place.

Rabies

Rabies is a disease of mammals which attacks the central nervous system and kills the infected person or animal within a few weeks. Rabies causes a horrible and painful death, characterized by extreme paranoia, ravings, and violent fits of temper. If you are bitten by a strange animal, you should never take chances. Wash the area with soap, water, and any disinfectant you have on hand, then call a doctor. If the animal which bit you cannot be found and certified free of the rabies virus, shots may have to be administered which, while painful, may ultimately save your life.

A unique mountain belief is that a stone cut from the stomach of a deer can draw rabies and other poisons from the body. In some parts of Appalachia, popular wisdom recommends that the stone first be soaked in a mixture of sulphur water, raw milk, and vinegar. Relax while you place the stone over the area where you were bitten to pull out the poison—then go see a doctor.

To protect yourself from being bitten by a rabid animal, carry a smooth black stone in your right pocket.

Shingles

Similar to chicken pox, shingles is a form of the herpes virus which attacks the skin and produces poison ivy-like blisters. Unlike chicken pox, shingles can attack the central nervous system and undermine the immune system, causing more dreaded diseases such as encephalitis and cancer.

At the first sign of shingles, take a bath in the blood of a black chicken whose body has been buried facing west. In Celtic mythology, the west was the direction of the land of the dead, and this spell may have been intended to symbolically "lay to rest" the disease.

Stomach Ache/Dyspepsia

While some abdominal discomforts can indicate a more serious condition, most of the time we hurt either because we ate too much or too well.

Medicinally, linden flower or chamomile teas are great for easing a tender stomach, and drinking water laced with wild mint or chewing on peppermint stems works well for an upset stomach or nausea.

A popular mountain antacid calls for eating a raw potato. (I tried this out of curiosity, and found it actually worked!)

Magickal cures for a belly ache include hanging rhubarb around your neck, sleeping under your bed instead of on it, rolling in a hay stack, or tying a live toad(*) to your side.

Sore Throat

Chewing calamus root(*) is a popular treatment for sore throat. Or you might make a syrup out of moonshine, red oak bark, sourwood honey, and wild berries, and take two tablespoons every two hours.

Amber beads worn around the neck for three days starting on an old (waning) moon will cure sore throat in two days' time.

Styes

A stye is an infection of the eyelid which can be very irritating, though it is not usually threatening, and will often go away on its own in about a week. Mountain folk believe that placing a wedding ring around the affected eye will speed the cure.

Surgery

The mountain folks have never liked operations, and even today many rural people will postpone or cancel needed surgery without apparent reason. The old-timers believe that the operation has the best chance of success if it can be scheduled when the moon is waning and/or is in the sign of Pisces or Aries.

Toothaches

Most toothaches are caused by plain old cavities which must eventually be treated by a dentist. In the meantime, place some vanilla extract on the tooth to stop the throbbing.

Sleeping on wet ashes is also supposed to affect a cure.

Tie some purslane to the side of your face affected, and run through a garden shouting "hurrah for the

Devil." Turn three times counterclockwise and spit on the ground. Bury the purslane.

Tremors

Tremors can be caused either by drunkenness or by certain illnesses such as Parkinson's Syndrome. Give jimson root for a medicinal cure or, for a magickal touch, take some scrapings from a cow's horn and some hairs from the arm of the affected person. Bind these together and take them to a graveyard at midnight. Bury them in the far northeast corner of the cemetery, then leave by the southwest side, without looking back.

Tumors/Cancer

Great strides in treating cancer have been made in the last few decades, but many folks have discovered a host of natural remedies which work very well as a supplemental treatment. The debate over natural treatments for cancer is heated and ugly, with many of those who have touted natural cures being run out of the country. Again, it is best to find a doctor sympathetic to natural remedies and allow him or her to use them in tandem with conventional treatments.

Sugar is removed from the diet of the victim in most natural regimes, but, in Appalachia, it is still believed that sweet sourwood honey and corn whiskey will help in healing.

Chickweed, which can be found all year in the southern mountains, has been used widely there to reduce the size of tumors.

Adding large amounts of nettles(*) to the diet is also believed to help cure cancer. Nettles are rich in vitamin C, a substance which has been repeatedly tested and found to work miracles in some cancer patients. Be aware that folks not raised with nettles in their diet may have a severe allergic reaction to them, similar to that of ingesting poison ivy. Several mountain healers have touted blue cohosh as a cancer cure-all.

A spell to cure cancer involves magickal substitution using the affected person's skin scrapings and toenail clippings. Take these to the cemetery in which you expect to be buried someday (or area where you expect your ashes to rest) and dig a hole with your right hand. With your left hand place the hair and clippings inside. Pricking a finger on your right hand, allow several drops of your blood to fall into the hole. Visualize the cancer flowing out of you into the hole. The idea is to trick the cancer into thinking that the hair and nails in the hole are really you, and inducing it to follow. Cover the hole and, before you leave, mark a big 'X' over the top of the spot with a forefinger. Walk away without looking back. Repeat the spell monthly until cured.

Ulcers

Okra and applesauce are often given to treat ulcers in the mountains.

To ease the pain, tie a piece of meat which has been soaked in buttermilk to your stomach.

Warts

There is lots of mountain lore concerning how to rid a person of warts. Sleeping with a slab of bacon over the wart will help speed healing. Or you could prick it and allow some blood to fall into a piece of meat, which you should then bury.

Washing with rainwater gathered in a hollow tree stump overnight is another well-known cure.

Dishrags which have been accidentally dropped or stolen from a neighbor make excellent magickal cures. Wipe the wart with these and bury the cloths somewhere off your own property.

Tying hair from a horse's tail around the wart will make it dissolve in a day or two.

By far the most common method of wart removal involves magick and beans (shades of Jack and the Beanstalk!). For any of these spells you will need to have as many beans as you have warts. Be sure to count carefully, or the magick will not work. Take a single bean and rub it on a wart—one bean to a wart, please—and place each in a bag which has been made or bought especially for this purpose. Take the bag out to the road and drop it without looking back. The one who finds it and looks into the bag will get your warts.

You can also plant the beans. As they grow, your warts will vanish. However, if any seed fails to sprout, the wart to which it was magickally linked will not go away and the spell will have to be repeated.

Selling the warts to a witch via the beans is a common cure, though I've never been able to imagine what any self-respecting witch would want with someone else's warts.

Yeast Infections

Three excellent douches can be made from water and herbs which are fairly effective against internal fungus.

1. Add pinches of the following in equal parts to eight ounces of water: marigold, goldenseal, hyssop, and fennel.
2. Mix 5 parts water to 1 part vinegar and add a little sage.
3. In water, brew 3 parts white oak bark, 2 parts yellow dock, 2 parts wintergreen, 3 parts witch hazel bark, and 1 part alum. Wait for the mixture to cool completely before using. (I have used this last one and found it works pretty well.)

Cure-Alls

In mountain lore, there are several medicinal and magickal actions which are believed to be effective against nearly any ailment. Certainly foremost among these are the use of home-brewed moonshine and sourwood honey. Old-timers will tell you there are few illnesses that will not benefit from a dose of either or both.

On the magickal side, cut a potato in half and rub it against the area where the illness is concentrated. After you feel it has absorbed the disease, put it back together by shoving a nail through it to hold it shut. Bury it as far from your home as is reasonable. As it decays, your illness will go away.

It was commonly accepted in Pagan Europe that the color black had great healing properties, because of its ability to absorb both heat and light. In Appalachia, we see remnants of that belief in the black cords or strings which are often tied around an affected area on a person, worn for a while, then burned. Black bark and dark herbs are the preferred healing catalysts when all else fails. However, black clothing and blankets are avoided because of their association in the mountains with funerals.

Two cure-alls which combine Pagan beliefs and Christian faith healing are also widely used. One is that any water collected on Ash Wednesday (the first day of Lent on the Christian calendar) will cure anything, when used in teas or as a wash. In Pagan Celtic times, dew was collected on Bealtaine (an ancient major holiday observed each May 1st) and was said to have similar properties.

The laying on of hands is another old Pagan practice which survives in Christian fundamentalism, and is alive and well in Appalachia. This involves placing one's hands on an afflicted person and, in magickal terms, sending one's own personal healing energy into the sick person. To do this takes practice in controlling the human energy field, and it is usually reserved for an experienced healer. The witches and ministers of Appalachia will use the same procedure, but call upon their God to affect the cure through them. Both methods are equally successful.

The mountaineers also have special cure-alls for children. The most popular of these is to pass the child three times through the branches of a forked tree. Others include the use of milk—sprinkling the body with dandelions that have been dipped in milk, immersion in carrot juice and milk baths, and feeding the sick child milk that has been boiled inside a pig's bladder.

Remote Healing

One of the greatest skills of the witch or granny woman is the ability to send forth their consciousness to a remote location to perform healing tasks. This hard-to-master art, known as astral projection, allows the spirit to roam free while the body is sleeping, with the projector retaining full conscious knowledge of the event. Numerous books are on the market which teach specific methods of astral projection, and all of them will work, though every person seems to have one way which works best for them.[4]

Because a complete course in astral projection does take an entire book, detailed instructions in this art lie far beyond the scope of this text. If you do not already have some rudimentary astral skills, you can begin to develop them by practicing lying completely still while focusing on being "out of yourself." Do this daily until your entire physical body becomes numb, and you will likely find that your consciousness will go elsewhere just to relieve the boredom!

Because astral projection occurs naturally in sleep, you may want to set your alarm clock to go off at various hours throughout the night. As soon as you awaken, try to immediately recall what you were dreaming about. You may discover that you were doing more than just dreaming, but that your mind was literally in another place where events were taking place which just may be verifiable. Once you are confident that astral projection is already happening to you without your conscious participation, you may be more easily able to harness your consciousness to the process.

After you are able to consciously achieve the "out-of-body" sensation, you can begin astral traveling by willing yourself to another locale. Sometimes you will be at your destination instantaneously, other times you will fly there watching the landscape move rapidly past you. If you are new to astral travel, it is best to start small. Go no further than the next room or next yard until you get used to the sensations; otherwise you might experience setbacks that will ruin your new magickal self-confidence.

Once your astral body can be successfully directed outward, you can take it into the presence of any sick person in the world and begin the remote healing process.

While in your astral consciousness, you may be able to see things which are otherwise invisible, so you should first stand back and observe the body for obvious signs of disease. These might appear as dark spots in the aura (the subtle light/energy field surrounding the body). If these are seen, lay your hands over them and mentally will the darkness to come into your hands. When you have absorbed as much of it as you can, place your hands on the floor and allow the disease to run out and be grounded. Repeat the process as needed until the aura is clear.

If you are aware of a physical problem in a specific part of the body, you can move your hands to that part and repeat the above process, whether or not you see a dark presence there. Place your hands over this spot and project healing energy. Visualize the energy in whatever way is most easy for you to see, or whichever way you think might best heal the patient. Studying the is most easy for you to see, or whichever way you think might best heal the patient. Studying the healing effects of color may be beneficial if you intend to pursue this calling.[5]

While in your astral consciousness, you may also see shapes hovering around the body which suggest people who may be known or unknown to you. These could either indicate the loving presence of someone who wishes the person well and is there to help just as you are, or it could point to someone who is wishing the illness on the person. You will have to use your own psychic feelers to decide just who is there for what purpose. If you truly feel someone is there for no good, raise your hands and will a blast of pure white light to shoot from your palms. This light should drive back the ill-wisher. When the presence is gone, go about the area and gather up in your hands any "thick spots" in the atmosphere or dark areas which may have been left behind. Ground them as described previously.

Lastly, will a beam of protective gold-white light to encompass the person you are trying to heal. This will set up a psychic barrier which will be hard for someone who wants to hurt that person again to penetrate, and will give the person's own immune system time to build itself up.

When you are finished with the healing tasks, will yourself to return to your body in full waking consciousness.

Astral projection takes practice, but with persistence, some measure of success should be achieved fairly quickly. Be aware that it can be a difficult skill to fully master, and that using this art for remote healing is a *very* advanced magickal technique. If you feel you have a gift for healing, it may well be worth your time to practice this ancient art.

Endnotes to Chapter 3

1. Several of these names were taken from fiction, others from scattered incidental passages in non-fiction works. For those interested in learning more about the nicknames of magickal plants from many

Magical Herbs (Llewellyn) and Ernst Lehner's *Folklore and Symbolism of Flowers, Plants and Trees* (Tudor Publishing).

2. The making of sourwood honey, and some of the lore surrounding it, is discussed in detail in *Foxfire 2* (Garden City, NY: Doubleday and Co., 1973).

3. The making of moonshine has both historical and economic implications to the mountain people which are much more complex than most people realize. For a greater understanding, look into any of the books on the economic problems of Appalachia (see Bibliography).

4. My two favorite books on astral projection are Melita Denning and Osborne Phillips' *Practical Guide to Astral Projection* (Llewellyn), and J. H. Brennan's *Astral Doorways* (Aquarian Press). Both have much practical material, are easy to understand, and approach the art from two entirely different perspectives.

5. Look into either Ted Andrew's *How To Heal With Color* (Llewellyn), or Reuben Amber's *Color Therapy* (Aurora).

CHAPTER FOUR

Weather Witching

Down in the valley, the valley so low,
Hang your head over, hear the wind blow.
Hear the wind blow, dear, hear the wind blow,
Hang your head over, hear the wind blow.
      —Traditional Mountain Song

For those familiar with the folk magick of weather, violent weather offers both a challenge and an opportunity. The challenge lies in correctly predicting or shaping the weather, and the opportunity lies in properly exploiting the atmospheric changes which magickal folk for centuries have believed create prime conditions for successful magick.

Mountain Beliefs about Meteorological Phenomena

High in the Appalachian mountains, the most dangerous and awe-inspiring weather phenomenon is lightning. From an isolated hilltop, the jagged slash of white ripping open the darkened sky is a breathtaking sight, a display of primeval power which rarely fails to hold those who see it enraptured. Like the medieval Europeans, the mountaineers have often believed that this rip in the sky opens a portal between two worlds of existence. To some, this is the door between the world of humans and that of heavenly spirits; to others it is the gate between heaven and the horrors of the underworld.

Because of the elevation in southern Appalachia (as high as 6,684 feet above sea level), people who do not take cover during storms risk being struck by lightning. It happens frequently, though a surprising number of hearty mountain folk live to tell about the experience. From that time forward, they are respected in the community as gifted folk with strange and wonderful powers. Sometimes the strike leaves them impervious to pain, eliminates the need for much sleep, or gives them the power of second sight or the ability to heal by touch.

Immediately after the strike, the dubiously blessed survivor is tossed into a mud bath to neutralize the harmful effects of the electricity. The red clay, which makes up a large percentage of the Appalachian soil, has been discovered to be a natural insulator and grounder. The person's body and behavior are then observed by the family, which looks for signs of change, both mental and physical. Sometime shortly thereafter, a local witch or granny woman will further study the victim to assess what paranormal powers have been bestowed by the storm. These might include such miracles as super-human strength, photographic memory, or something as ordinary as a small scar which indicates a part of the body that has been given magickal ability.

Blizzards are not uncommon at these higher elevations, even in states we think of as being largely immune to heavy snowfalls. While winter and its snows are viewed by mountaineers as part of the natural cycle of time, blizzards have occasionally been seen as punishments meted out on a community by an unhappy God. The steep slopes of the mountains are treacherous in snow, and blizzards can make them outright deadly.

Tornadoes also occasionally hit the mountains, though they tend to skip over most homes since these are most often tucked into valleys where the bottoms of the funnels don't reach as they skim over the higher ridges. To the mountain mind, these cyclonic storms are the greatest manifestation of evil that nature can hand out, with the possible exception of epidemics.

Predicting the Weather

No matter how far modern technology takes us, we still have little control over our weather—even with magickal assistance. All we can really do is be on the lookout for signs of its approach, protect ourselves from the worst, and work with the best. Many of the weather portents known to Appalachia apply equally well throughout most of North America, others are based on folklore unique to the mountains. Use these guidelines as a sound basis for your own collection of predictions, but always be alert for other signs which may be unique to your area of the world.

Appalachian Weather Omens

When it is going to rain, cows will lie down in the fields, birds will fly low overhead, and locusts will sing. If the top of the tallest mountain in view is shrouded by clouds, the rain will appear within six hours. If the mountaintop is visible, expect the rain in eight to twelve hours time.

Chickens hovering near open doorways, and trees turning the undersides of their leaves upward also herald rain. Pigs will gather their young beneath them if an exceptionally heavy rain is approaching.

Winds blowing strong from the southeast herald a drenching rain, possibly a tropical storm. Winds from the southwest are always the strongest, and are potentially cyclonic.

If it rains on the day of the summer solstice, it will be an especially rainy summer, one during which you should be alert to flooding. If it rains on the spring equinox, look for a summer drought instead.

If the sun rises red, the weather that day is likely to be violent. If it sets red, look for a dry night.

If you see a burrowing animal frantically digging at midday, it forecasts a tornado within three hours' time. Dogs whimpering while turning in circles, or horses stamping at the edge of their corrals are other indications of an approaching cyclone.

Green-tinted skies to the southwest are a sign that a tornado or hail storm is fast approaching. Yellow-tinted skies herald an electrical storm, and gray-tinted skies, a gentle rain.

February 14, known to most of us as Valentine's Day, is officially Groundhog Day in Appalachia, rather than February 2, the date it is observed in the rest of the United States (selected because of its links to a Celtic Pagan festival honoring the Goddess Brighid). On this day the groundhog will come out of his den and either see his shadow, in which case the mountain folk have to endure six more weeks of winter, or he will not see a shadow and emerge from his den heralding an early spring. If other burrowing animals appear above ground between February 14 and March 1, it indicates an early spring.

It will be an especially hot summer if animals shed their winter coats before the first day of May, or if spring storms have lots of low, rumbling thunder with little or no lightning. It will be a cool summer if the night skies are mostly clear in May.

Whenever poison ivy turns red before the first of August, or when you notice excessive spider activity the first week in September, count on an early autumn.

An early and severe winter is indicated by a thick berry harvest in September, and this should be taken as a sign to load up on winter food stores.

If, by early September, animals cease their summer shedding, if snakes are no longer seen in the woods, or if field mice or earth worms enter homes and cabins seeking shelter, an early winter is at hand. Wide and/or numerous black bands on the backs of woolly worms, or crickets observed resting on their backs, are other signs of early winter.

The first killing frost should arrive precisely three months after the first katydid is heard in the late summer trees. If the apple harvest comes more than two weeks earlier than normal, a sharp frost will occur within three weeks.

It will be an especially harsh and cold winter if squirrels begin gathering food in late July, or if birds are seen gathering feed from the ground near your house.

Owls who make sounds more like crying humans than birds are a sign of a serious winter to come, as is chimney smoke which does not rise in the sky, but instead seems to settle down around your home.

Snow will come within three days' time, should a winter fire made of dry wood pop when lit. If the fire causes tapping noises to come from up the chimney flue, a blizzard is likely.

From the mountains of Georgia comes a forecast which says that if you count the number of days which you are into either the new or old moon at the time of the first snow, that it foretells how many other times it will snow that winter. For instance, if the first snow comes on the fourth day of the moon's waning cycle, expect four more snows that season. Or if the first snow comes on the second day of the moon's waxing cycle, expect two more snows before spring.

Making Weather Happen

Crafting the weather is an ancient magickal art, a skill which has always been attributed to witches, wizards, and other magickal people. In medieval Europe, it was a capital crime to magickally tamper with the natural patterns of weather. There are extant drawings from that period showing witches gleefully brewing up storms of all kinds in order to make mischief.[1] Interestingly, the figures are always shown as female, even though many male magicians, including the Celtic Druids (a largely male priesthood), were reputed to be highly skilled in weather magick. In fact, it was the Druids who were credited with creating the sea storm which wrecked the attacking Spanish Armada in 1588.

In Appalachia, there is still a persistent belief that women are the natural weather witches, and it is considered very bad luck for a woman to go about whistling. This is directly linked to the old process of "whistling up a wind," an art which both witches and Witches still practice today.

In the southern mountains, weather magick is the sole province of witches and granny women, and most of their secrets have been carefully guarded. By drawing on Anglo-Celtic magickal practices, mountain folktales, and reports of what mountain folk have observed their witches doing, it is relatively easy to extrapolate the essence of the practices. However, be warned that weather magick is an art all its own, one which takes many years to master. It also implies a great responsibility as your actions will affect many other lives.

Before attempting any weather magick, you will need to spend some quality time allowing yourself to get to know the weather, to learn to sense its presence within yourself. Almost everyone has some type of reaction to certain kinds of weather, responses which they instantly recognize. For example, do you have an old injury that aches whenever the barometric pressure starts to drop? Does your hair stand on end when a cold, dry spell is upon you? Do you feel energized just before a storm blows in, or restless and blue before a big snow? All these are very common reactions to explainable atmospheric changes, and are a useful place to start your exploration.

Fine-tuning your psyche and body to the more subtle ebbs and flows of the weather is a bit harder, but necessary to mastering this difficult art. Spend at least fifteen minutes daily sitting outdoors, or near an open window, allowing yourself to commune with the current weather pattern. Make notes if you need them to help you remember what you are sensing. If you are serious about weather magick, you may want to begin a weather journal, recording your feelings and discoveries as you study. For example, if it is raining, try to memorize, and/or record, all the sensations you feel: the sight, the smell, the sound, the very *frequency* on which the rain functions. Then, later on, like tuning in the proper wave length on your radio when you want your favorite station, you will be able to tune in to the rain when you want it again.

Be especially sensitive to sounds which different weather patterns stir within you. These are the voices of the weather, and by learning these sounds you can call to mind your desired weather pattern, and actually be heard by it. As the weather and you become one, start humming a single note, moving up and down the scale until you find a tone which seems to match the melody of the weather. When you discover this, memorize it and/or make a note of it in your magickal diary or weather notebook. Also note the direction from which the weather pattern hails, as each compass point can have its own distinct sound and feel even though its product appears to be the same.

If all this preparation sounds difficult, it can be, which is why, in Appalachia, weather shaping is the sole province of experienced magickians.

Unlike many kinds of weather, a wind rarely has any serious repercussions on people. Calling up a wind is probably the most common form of weather magick found in the repertoire of any modern magickian. The direction from which the wind blows is essential to certain spells which depend upon the alchemical element of air for their success. West winds are usually used for magick related to death, childbirth, and fertility; and north winds are for spells relating to the home, peace, and repose. Winds from the east are often called upon for matters of new ventures, education, and communication; and south winds are for protection and for stirring the passions.

Once you have the wind you want, you can use it for magick in any of several ways.[2] You can blow or toss magickally charged herbs into the wind, set out a magickally empowered bell to catch the breeze and release the magick for you, or allow writings—such as those on a scrap of lightweight paper or carved in soil with a stick—which symbolize something you no longer want in your life to be blown away. Winds can also be useful for cleansing the psychic air near your home, turning a brush fire away from inhabited areas, or for making any of the wind-specific magick mentioned above.

There are two techniques for stirring up the wind which are still known today. One involves whistling or calling out to the wind, and the other utilizes a whip.

The whistling/calling out method was revived in modern Witchcraft through the efforts of the late Sybil Leek, a hereditary Pagan from England who went public about her faith in the 1950s, after Britain repealed its long-standing anti-witchcraft laws. In 1967, while on a visit to San Francisco, Sybil was challenged to prove her powers as a Witch by stirring up a wind. On a calm day, a local reporter went with her to the waterfront and watched as she worked her wind spell. Within a few seconds after her call, a brisk wind swept in from over the Bay.[3]

To call the wind, start by standing on the highest point you can safely find, facing the direction from which you wish the wind to come. It helps if you have a fair amount of open ground around you, since buildings, trees, etc., can impede your sense of the wind. In other words, you may succeed in calling it, but you may never know this if it can't get to you. Raise your arms upward and outward to the direction you face, palms facing outward. Or, if you prefer, you may hold a magickal tool, such as a wand, in one hand, though bear in mind that this is not a part of the Appalachian experience. With your mind, reach out to the wind, visualize yourself making contact with it to the farthest corners of the earth. Then make the sound which you have discovered goes with the particular wind you wish to call. Allow the sound to rise slowly in your throat, building to a piercing cry as if you are trying to project your voice over vast miles. If you can do this all in one breath, so much the better, though beginners may find this hard to do at first.

When you feel the wind has heard your cry, peal out three sharp whistles, just as loud as you can make them. Or call forth with three sharp hoots. Then, with your arms still raised and spread, fall silent and wait to feel that first exhilarating brush of breeze to come rushing at you.

If you are using a whip (any three-foot length of medium-weight rope will work very well as a substitute) to call the wind, you will need plenty of room in which to wield it safely.

Again, stand outdoors facing the direction from which you want the wind to come, and mentally feel your connection with that wind. Allow the sound of the wind you want to build in you as before, but this time begin to twirl the whip high above your head in a rapid counterclockwise spin. Make sure the whip or rope is moving fast and steady so that it produces an even-toned whistling noise in the air. If you can make it hum at the frequency of the wind you want, all the better. When you sense that the wind has heard you, stop twirling and crack the whip in front of you with the loudest pop you can make, just as if you were ordering about a circus tiger. Then stand still and wait for the wind to respond.

If you find you have no talent or patience for calling up a wind, you can still magickally capture it to work for you at a later time. An ancient technique for capturing the wind is to tie it up in a rope by using knots.[4] Any rope of three to six feet in length should be enough. You might want to color-coordinate each of your ropes to match the traditional colors of the directions. For instance, you might choose red or orange for the south, blue or silver for the west, brown or green for the north, or white or yellow for the east. When a good, brisk wind is coming from the direction of your choice, take your rope and head outdoors.

Hold your rope in both hands and stand facing into the wind. Call out a greeting such as:

> *Wind of the* (insert direction),
> *I have eagerly awaited your coming.*
> *Welcome to this land.*
> *It is blessed by your presence.*

If you work your magick within a Judeo-Christian framework, you may want to change the last line of that greeting so that you are thanking your God for the blessing of the wind, rather than following the more Pagan model of thanking the wind for bringing its own blessing. Either way is effective.

You should have decided in advance how many knots you wish to use. Usually this is a number sacred to your own magickal tradition. In Appalachia, the numbers three or seven are most often used. Three because of its Celtic associations, and seven because of Biblical references, the origin of the expression "lucky seven."

To capture the wind's power, hold a section of the rope up and feel the wind rushing it, charging it with magickal power, and say something such as:

> *Wind of the* (insert direction), *elusive and free,*
> *Come into this rope to work for me.*
> *My needs are great, my intentions pure,*
> *As I tie this knot, your help I secure.*

Still holding the rope above your head, tie a quick, snug knot in it, visualizing the wind being captured there. Then repeat this process for as many knots as you wish to make.

When you want to utilize the magick of the wind, take your rope to your working place and untie a single knot just as you reach the climax of your spell, more if you feel the need for an extra boost of air magick. You may even be rewarded with a faint breeze from the wind's direction, reaffirming your spell's success.

Keep the charged ropes in a dark place when not in use, preferably in pouches where they will not touch each other, or come into contact with your other magickal tools. This is so that they will remain uncontaminated by other energies, and retain their power.

Though clearly harder to manifest than the wind, rain making has a noble history, one which modern magickal folk should hope to reclaim. Making rain come when needed is a form of weather magick which has consumed humankind for millennia. The Jews have a special prayer for rain which is recited each autumn, as it has been for thousands of years, and in drought-ridden areas of the Bible Belt, Christian groups will often gather to pray the dry spell away. Native Americans have become famous for their successful rain dances, and many of the Pagan fertility rites of old Europe were deeply concerned with bringing rains.

The basic Appalachian technique for evoking rain uses a long stick or branch, probably a descendant of the Pagan magick wand, and a small cup or bowl. Noon is the traditional time for rain-making spells in North America, but you should choose the time you feel you can best attune to the weather pattern.

Start by standing alone outside, facing the direction from which rain is most likely to come to your area. Throw your head back as if rain were falling in your face, and allow your mind to attune to the frequency of rain. You may hum or sing if it helps you make this connection. Then raise the stick above your head and begin spinning it counterclockwise, the same direction as the air moves in the low pressure system necessary for rain. Visualize the end of the stick extending far into the heavens churning and stirring the sky into the pattern you need for rain making.

When you feel your spell has been successful, or when you feel you have done all you can for one session, quit by lowering the stick and tapping it on the ground in front of you three times. As mentioned in a previous chapter, three taps on the ground is an intricate part of many ancient Anglo-Celtic evocation spells. You may repeat the spell again later in the day, or the next day, if needed.

End the rain-making spell by setting out a cup or bowl in which to catch the rain. This is an act of faith in your magick by which you are saying, "Alright, now I've done it, and I believe so much in my power that I am setting out these receptacles to catch the product of my magick."

Following in the tradition of Native Americans, some mountain witches, as well as many other magickians, have created their own rain dances, with varying degrees of success. If this idea appeals to you, by all means give it a try. You may discover a new talent.

Magickal Protection from Violent Weather

Magickally shielding one's self and one's home from tornadoes, lightning, and hail are the most common forms of protective weather magick known anywhere on the planet, and such practices are very common in Appalachia.

If lightning is threatening you and you find yourself outdoors, you should first take all non-magickal, common sense precautions such as getting out from under tall objects like telephone poles and trees, and trying to make yourself as flat and low to the ground as possible.

Magickally protecting yourself from lightning when you are outdoors usually requires some advance planning. Carrying geranium petals in your pockets is one popular remedy against being struck, and is said to protect you from snakebite as well.

Using a branch from a tree which has been struck by lightning in the past as a walking stick is a method that is sworn upon by many mountaineers. This is another example of magickal substitution based on the widely held belief that lightning will never strike twice in the same spot. By carrying something with you which has already been struck, it is expected that you will be safe from a second strike.

Knocking one white stone against one black one until you are safely indoors is supposed to set up magick currents of protection around you which lightning cannot penetrate.

There is always a chance that lightning may cause a fire if it strikes your home or land, and direct strikes are not uncommon at higher elevations. Fortunately it is usually damp in Appalachia, and the sort of lightning fires which have been known to wipe out thousands of acres in the American West are rare, but occasionally they do occur.

To protect your home from a lightning fire, hang a small bag over your front door containing chips from a tree which has previously been struck by lightning. Or you can take four bark chips of equal size and bury them outside at each corner of your home, encircling it with protective energy. Like the walking stick idea, these are two more examples of magickal substitution.

Flint, a bedrock which has been used for over 30,000 years to strike sparks and create fire, is also used for lightning protection when the rocks are placed in all four corners of the home. Go about the house clockwise as you do this, beginning your journey in the east, the most common direction by which rains come into the mountains.

Keeping a fire going in your home during a storm, either in the form of an oil lamp, candle, or hearth fire is another protection based on magickal substitution. In this case, a fire is already burning at your home, so any lightning seeking to make a fire there will see the job has already been done and will look elsewhere to cause trouble.

If you can induce a family of barn swallows to take up residence in your barn or other outbuilding, lightning will never strike them.

In Celtic Europe, mistletoe was heavily used as a protection against lightning strikes. The mountain people share this perception, but believe that in order for it to be effective, the mistletoe must grow naturally on the property and not be brought in by humans. Carried in your pockets, or hung in your home or barn, it will release its protective energies. Some Appalachian farmers have been known to tie the sprigs to the halters of their cows who, while grazing in high-elevation open fields, are frequently targets of lightning. In general, using mistletoe to protect your animals is not recommended, since the berries are toxic.

Tornadoes and hail storms create their own kind of danger to property, people, and animals. Large hailstones can kill people and livestock, tear off roofs, and destroy crops. Tornadoes, as we all know, can destroy anything and everything standing in their paths. Common sense is always the best approach for dealing with these two dangerous weather phenomena. At the first sign of trouble, take cover in a basement or inside room, away from windows. If you have time, cover your car with a heavy tarp or place it in a garage, and make sure pets and livestock are sheltered.

To magickally protect your home from tornadoes, place a sharp knife in the ground on the southwest corner of your property, or in a window which faces southwest. Since most tornadoes travel from southwest to northeast, the knife can meet the cyclone as it approaches and magickally divide the funnel, driving it to the sides of your house rather than through it. Or you can divert the cyclone away from an inhabited area by placing several knives across the southwest boundary of the area you wish it to pass over. You can also place a large cauldron or barrel on the same southwest corner. The dark abyss of the cauldron is believed to be confusing to the tornado and it may get its tail caught inside and be dissipated before reaching your home.

Planting geraniums on the southwestern edge of your land is also a mountain protection from storms, one which is pretty to look at as well.

If a tornado is likely to come your way, take a moment to place the palm of your right hand against a window pane and utter a charm or prayer such as:

> *Wind born of evil, spinning fast,*
> *Jump this place, move on, go past.*

Finish by marking a giant 'X' over the glass with your finger and walk away without looking out that window again until the danger has passed. However, if a tornado has actually been sighted near your home, stay as far away from the windows as possible since the intense low pressure of the storm can cause the glass to shatter and blow inward.

It is believed that tornadoes will pass by any dwelling which shelters a hog. In fact, there were once so many protective reasons to bring swine into the home that, until well into this century, it was not uncommon in Appalachia to find a pig or two sharing human abodes. Though few today can remember all the reasons why this was done, the practice can probably be traced to a medieval belief in cloven-hooved animals as servants of the Devil,[5] just as is the tornado itself is considered to be. In other words, the tornado will not want to go after one of its own, and will pass over the hog's dwelling place.

To shield your home from hail damage, toss acorns onto your roof just as it begins to rain.

A Word to the Wise Magickian about Storms

Pagan Europe has bequeathed to us the tradition of magick being eagerly worked during storms. The mixture of rain, wind, and lightning pounding the earth not only creates potent, raw energy from which we can draw power, but it also gives us the four alchemical elements with which to work, the building blocks with which our ancestors believed all things were created—including magick. During a storm you have rain (water), wind (air), lightning (fire) all pummeling the land (earth) on which you live.

Those of you who choose to work outdoors to harness storm magick must use extra caution, especially if you employ metal tools in your work. In any case, it is best to come inside just before the center of the storm is upon you. Counting the seconds between the lightning flash and the sound of thunder which follows is a good indication of just how close the storm is to you. The shorter the count, the closer the storm. Since light travels faster than sound, you may assume the storm is about one-half mile away for each full second you count between boom and flash. Also, keep an eye on the immediate horizon; if the lightning appears to be striking the ground, go inside and work your magick from there.

If tornadoes or hurricanes are in the forecast, you should be doubly cautious. At the first sign of serious, violent weather, such as the spotting of a funnel cloud, go inside and take immediate cover.

Working with the raw elements of nature can be rewarding for the serious student of magick, but it is never worth the risk of being hurt or killed.

Endnotes to Chapter 4

1. For example, see Ernst and Johanna Lehner's *Picture Book of Devils, Demons and Witchcraft* (Dover, 1971), p. 59, plate 84; or p. 70, plate 102.

2. For more on working with wind magick, though from a non-Appalachian perspective, see Scott Cunningham's *Earth Power* or *Earth, Air, Fire and Water* (both Llewellyn).

3. Leek, Sybil. *The Complete Art of Witchcraft* (New York: Signet Books, 1971).

4. A sixteenth-century engraving of a sorcerer selling wind tied up in knots to sailors can be found in Lehner, p. 69, plate 99.

5. This acceptance of cloven-hooved animals, particularly swine, as evil beings comes from a corruption of the Euro-Asian Pagan religions wherein these animals were sacred to many of the old Goddesses. One of the best known examples is the Celtic sow Goddess, Cerridwen.

CHAPTER FIVE

Of Home, Hearth, and Earth

It's home, daughter, home, it's here you ought to be,
It's home, daughter, home, in your own country.
Where oak, ash, and pine, and the fine willow tree,
All are growing green in North Ameriky.
—Traditional Mountain Ballad
adapted from an English Folk Song

Today all types of homes, reflecting a myriad of lifestyles and incomes, can be found in the southern Appalachians, especially in its cities and larger communities. But in the not-too-distant past clapboard cabins and frame homes handcrafted from native woods were the norm. Many of these cabins still stand and are used as primary dwellings in the more isolated reaches of the range. Unlike the log homes found in the upper third of North America, which are Scandinavian in origin, the mountain people's Celtic forebears most likely learned the art of cabin making from the Cherokee, who learned it from French fur trappers sometime in the early eighteenth century. While the Scandinavian style homes used whole logs, precisely stacked and interlocked with each other, the Appalachian homes more often used wood planking. The result was thinner outside walls, but ones which used less wood and required less planning to coordinate all the pieces.

The Magickal Mountain Home

As in Europe, home ownership in the mountains came with many omens, taboos, and magickal opportunities; some of them pertaining to the dwelling itself, others concerning the land or the tasks performed there. Many magickal protection rites for the home are still observed in the mountains, even though the original meaning of most of these rituals has been forgotten. This is rather like people today refusing to walk under a ladder. No one can explain just why we don't like to do it, but most of us won't if it can be avoided.

Like their Celtic ancestors, mountain people built their cabins around a central hearth, which was literally the heart of the home.[1] The fireplaces were used not only for home heating, cooking, gathering, storytelling, but for making magick as well. Sadly, so many modern homes and apartments no longer contain a fireplace. If you have no hearth for these spells, you can use a candle, censer, or heat-resistant bowl left burning as near to the center of your home as possible.

The Scottish immigrants to Appalachia brought with them the European belief of the chimney flue as a magickal opening to the home, one which must be carefully guarded. European folklore records for us numerous tales of witches flying up chimneys on enchanted brooms, of benevolent house sprites who take up residence near the hearth, and of sinister beings who use the flue to enter the home in spirit and wreak their havoc.[2] Fortunately, the immigrants also brought with them a host of magickal remedies for these problems.

A pot of some sort must always be kept warm on the hearth to catch and destroy any evil which might come down the chimney. In Pagan Europe, the pot often took the form of a cauldron, the cauldron being symbolic of the womb of the great Mother Goddess, through which all things must pass as they are born and to which they must return upon death. Recall the folktale of *The Three Little Pigs*, whose climax comes when the Big Bad Wolf crawls down the chimney with the intention of eating the pigs for dinner. His evil plot is thwarted when he falls into the waiting cauldron and is killed.

When a cauldron is set to boil in the hearth, it will not only keep unwanted things out, but will keep good things from escaping from your home through the flue. This is thought to be especially useful if someone fears their spirit is being "called out" nightly by a witch. Hanging implements made of iron over the hearth is another ancient protective practice of Celtic origin.

Burning oak logs in the hearth strengthens the home against natural disasters, pine and cedar logs bring it prosperity, birch wood brings happiness, and elm protects it from curses and other evil intents. Tossing basil or rosemary into the fire also protects and brings happiness.

Black smoke coming from a chimney is an omen that a curse has been levied on the home, gray smoke speaks of a quarrel to come between two who live under the roof, and white smoke announces to all that this is a clean and happy dwelling. Golden sparks spraying from the hearth fire mean good times ahead, but hissing sounds are a sign of bad times to come.

Items grouped together to utilize the power of the Celtic sacred number "three" are also used as fireplace protections. These might include ideas such as drawing three circles or crosses over the hearth opening, hanging three groupings of protective herbs (like basil, rosemary, and rue), tacking up three metal pans, etc.

Heating a fireplace tool, or even a long stick, in the hearth, and then taking it outdoors to draw a clockwise circle on the ground around your home, will protect it from any unwelcome influence or spirit which might seek entry. The clockwise circle is an ancient protective practice dating back before recorded history, one which is still used by Witches and other magickians for protecting themselves when practicing lengthy spells or religious rites.

Casting salt water about your home is another excellent way to protect it, a method taken directly from Pagan Europe. Asperging an area with salted water is often done to purify magick circles in modern Witchcraft. As you go about your home with the water, you might want to chant a charm such as the one on page 95.

> *Water and salt cast out the sin,*
> *Blessings to take their place come in.*

Brooms were also important magickal tools in Europe, and they have retained some of that essence in the mountains. Often a broom will rest by the fireplace like a guardian spirit, or be used to sweep evil influences out the door as soon as they are suspected.

Since nothing which is evil can cross over a prone broomstick, brooms are often laid lengthwise across the hearth opening so that nothing wicked which finds its way down the chimney can enter the house proper. As you lay the broom in place, empower it with a charm such as:

> *Broomstick guard this opening wide,*
> *None uninvited may come inside.*

Brooms take an interest in their home and should never be loaned out to someone else. You invite disaster if you change residences and take the old broom with you. Brooms are also territorial, and you should never allow anyone else to bring another broom into your home for cleaning purposes. This admonition seems rather odd when taken at face value, since the belief is specifically amended to include "cleaning purposes" only. This has to make one wonder why anyone would tote a broom around with them unless the stricture was deliberately leaving room for brooms to be used as magickal tools when brought to home coven gatherings by Witches.

In the Blue Ridge region of Virginia, some folks still swear that a piece of blue glass can turn away the "evil eye." The evil eye is a popular name for a curse taken from a story in Irish mythology about the God Balor, who had an eye so horrible that it took ten men to help him get it open, and whomever his gaze then fell upon would die. Several Irish folktales still exist, such as that of Biddy Early, which tell of wise women who kept magickal protection spells in blue bottles. Hence, blue glass is often found sitting on Appalachian windowsills to repel curses.

Window openings are sometimes protected with sprigs of fresh rosemary, basil, or woodruff, all herbs which have the added benefit of imparting a nice woodsy fragrance in the house when caught by a breeze. Broken glass is also used as a home protection device for windows. The shards are collected and placed in canning jars or other transparent vials and left on the sill to "cut and slice" at anything uninvited trying to enter.

While broken mirrors have also been used as window protection in other cultures, the mountain folk never keep their broken mirror glass around. In fact, a broken mirror is viewed as a strong magnet for attracting evil, and must be disposed of after the curse is first broken by touching each of the largest shards to the oldest headstone in a graveyard at midnight.

Mountain protection rites for the door portal—commonly called the threshold—also come from Britain and the Celtic lands. The threshold was not always the name applied to an entire door, but was once the specific name for a strip of wood which kept the precious grain on a threshing house floor from falling out. Because of the sacred connotations of grain (fertility, prosperity, abundance, etc.) the object which held it in place naturally acquired its own magickal significance and had to be protected as well. Even if no other part of a mountain house is scrupulously clean, the door is scrubbed daily, an act of sympathetic magick to attract good things to the home.

Dried leather beans, called "breeches beans," are often strung together on string and hung over the door to bring good luck and protection to the home. This is an example of sympathetic magick, the magick of attraction, which presumes that if food is hanging around available in the dwelling, then the family need never do without.

Iron has always been reputed to have the power to repel unwanted faery life, and it is used above both doors and fireplace mantles to keep these unseen beings from entering.[3] Horseshoes made of iron, time-honored good luck symbols from Ireland, are placed above doorways to bless the opening.

A squeaky door hinge is an invitation to troublesome spectral beings, and should be greased down with lard as soon as possible. A squeaky floorboard just inside the door must be removed and replaced with all due haste if you don't want to attract vermin, but if you have a squeaky board just outside your door you should leave it be, as its noise will scare away unwanted entities which approach your door.

Urine mixed with vinegar and used to wash the front door will make your home burglar proof! If you like the idea of a "piss and vinegar" spell, but would like a more sanitary method of applying it, try using a small, disposable cup to contain and keep the mixture in a safe location in your bathroom. Its protective energies will work just as well for you there.

Placing a saucer over the front door will turn away a would-be thief, and ferns or ivy growing on your front porch will turn away a curse. However, if an animal destroys the plant first, then it means a curse is already in place on your home. If you wish to hedge your bets with this spell, a pot of dill growing on the porch will drive away animal predators.

Magick at Your Feet

Unique to Appalachia are the many household omens and magickal practices surrounding shoes. Until after World War II (1939–1945), shoes were a precious and rare commodity in the mountains, a fact which gave rise to the stereotypical image of the barefoot hillbilly stomping around the woods on his huge, leathery feet. Because of this scarcity, shoes were cherished as a sign of prosperity and were often hung suspended on rope near the hearth or nailed up over the front door so that other good things would come in after them.

Being gifted with a used pair of shoes from someone who possesses demonstrable good fortune will allow you to walk in that same path. Because shoes are most often handed down from older to younger siblings, there is a great responsibility to set a "good example" placed on older children's shoulders.

Wearing the shoes of someone who is not doing so well for himself should be avoided, or you could be dragged into his or her endless cycle of failures.

Once someone dies, any shoes which belonged to that person must be destroyed and not worn by anyone ever again, no matter how nice or new they may be. To do so only invites death to take the wearer.

Shoes must never be placed on tables or beds. Aside from the fact that this is less than sanitary, it will bring terrible misfortune to the one who is so careless.

Company's Comin'

Company is always a welcome diversion in the isolated hills, so naturally there are several ways to ascertain just when visitors are coming, the nature and needs of those visitors, and, if company is not in your future, ways to magickally draw some to your door.

If your dog chooses to sleep in the front doorway of your home, you may expect a visitor that day. Accidentally dropping your flatware means you can expect company which will need to be fed. If you sneeze upon awakening, it means a cherished friend will arrive before sundown, but if you sneeze upon going to bed at night, a stranger will come of whom you should be wary. A rocking chair which travels across the floor as it is being rocked is another omen that your family should be cautious in dealings with strangers.

Dropping beans on the floor is an indication that friends who have not been seen in a long time will soon be heard from.

Mountain cabins often have a back door directly opposite the front door, which will allow someone standing out front to see clear through the house and out the back again. These are known as "shotgun homes," named because a gun could be fired into one door and safely exit the other without risking hitting someone in between. Such home designs are practical if you expect to be feuding with your neighbors on a regular basis, but they also have their magickal uses. If you see no portents of visitors in your future, and you wish to have some, then open both your front and back doors and run **in** the front and **out** the back nine times in succession (if you have no back door, substitute an inner-door of some kind for this spell). As you run, you may want to chant a charm such as:

> *In one door and out the other,*
> *Come neighbor, friend, or kin, or brother.*
> *Heed my magick and need my face,*
> *Company appear now at this place.*

If your right palm itches, it means welcome company will soon be at your door. If the left palm itches, you will soon be faced with visitors you would rather not see.

If you have guests who are overstaying their welcome, attempt to get them to walk out the front door on some pretense, and then have them come back in to the house through the back door. After doing this they will suddenly be taken with the urge to go home.

Or you can remove them by casting a rock in through the back door and out the front while saying:

> *No walls can hold the restless one,*
> *Company come, company gone.*

As long as the rock goes clear through the home on the first toss without hitting anything inside, and as long as your company remains unaware of the spell, it will be successful.

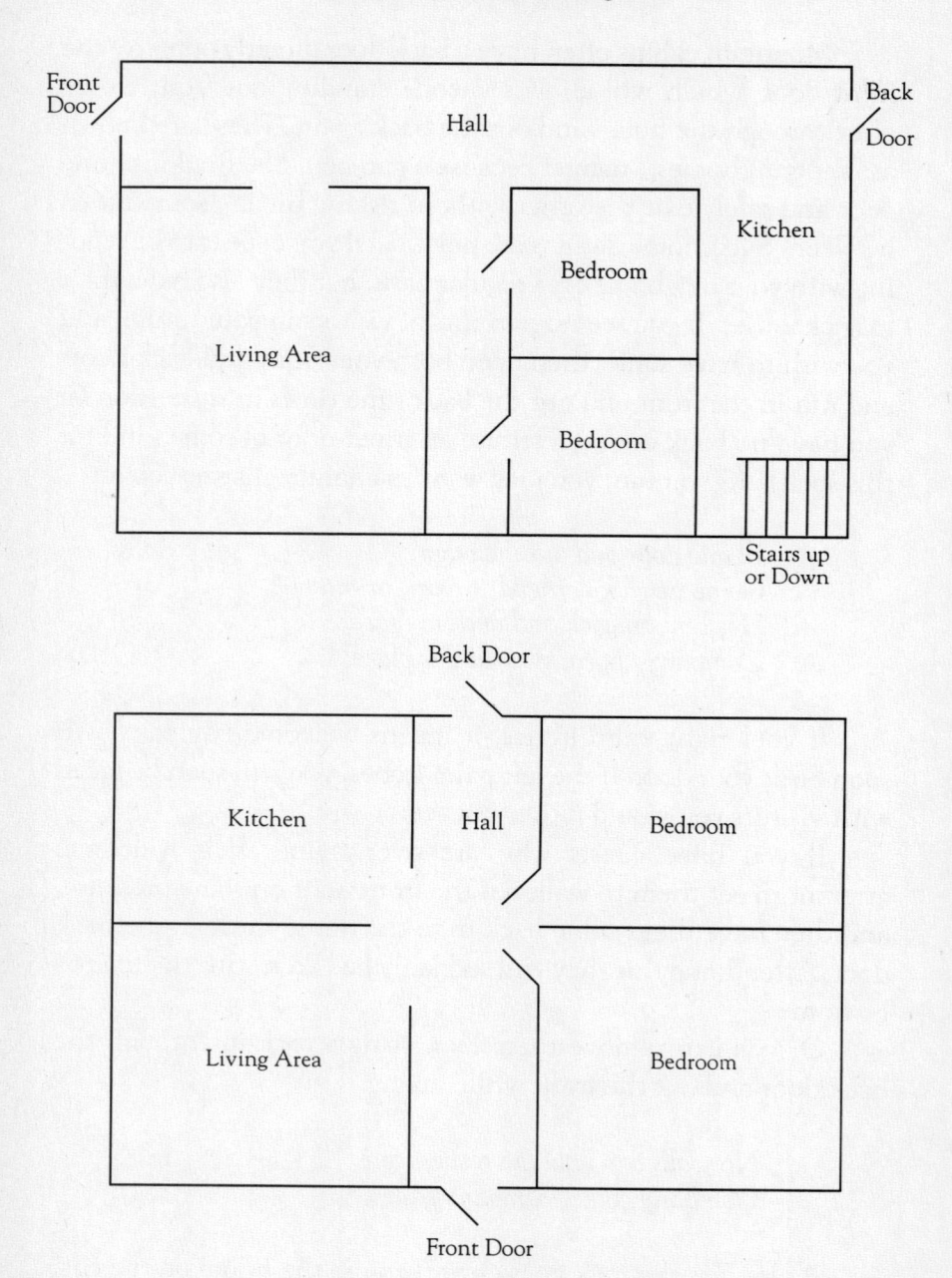

Two versions of the shotgun floor plan.

Feuding Omens and Family Peace Magick

Feuds between rival clans are well-known and documented in southern Appalachia, some of the more famous ones having been carried on for several generations. Like all families everywhere, mountain folk also have to contend with inner-household squabbles which can be upsetting for everyone. Fortunately, there are omens and magickal remedies for many of these instances.

If a weapon is dropped on the floor while indoors, or falls from its wall mounting, it foretells a quarrel between your household and another. If, as it falls, it lands on someone who lives in the house, then it is an omen of an upcoming inner-family dispute.

Strange stars appearing over your home are an indication that you will be embroiled in a feud before the next new moon. A chair which breaks when sat in is another sign of a quarrel to come with another family.

With family loyalty being very high on the mountaineers' list of values, it is considered very important to stop inner-family squabbles before they get out of hand. After the entire household is asleep under one roof, the person wishing to stop the quarrel should take salt water to each person's bedside and, without their knowing it, anoint the forehead while whispering words such as:

Anger be gone, peace now reign,
One happy family we begin again.

Placing lodestones, rocks with magnetic properties, underneath the mattresses of the quarreling parties will also draw them together again.

If you can get nail clippings from the two warring factions, you should powder them and place them in a drink which you give to both parties first thing in the morning. The fight should end by sundown.

Quarrels which go on indefinitely, or which cause one party to move from the residence, must be dealt with by stronger magick. Take nail clippings or other small items belonging to each of the parties and wrap them together in a pink or white cloth (both colors of peace and purity). Tie the bundle with blue string (for loyalty) and take it to the graveyard at midnight. Place the bundle on top of the headstone of your oldest ancestor who is buried there, or simply use the oldest grave if you have no family nearby, and set some bread down beside the stone. Walk away without looking back. The quarrel should end in three days' time.[4]

Magickal Foods and Dining Taboos

Arguably, the most important spice ever discovered by humankind was salt, a substance which has been used in magick for many centuries. It has been used as a preservative, a flavor enhancer, and magickally as a source of protection and grounding. Perhaps this is why so many cultures have omens and taboos dealing with salt. In Appalachia, salt must never be passed from person to person around the dinner table, but must be placed back down on the board and each person who wants it must pick it up again. If the salt is spilled, a portion of it must be tossed out the window.

Salt and bread are the first items which must be brought into a new cabin, so that they will magickally bring prosperity with them. If a family ever allows itself to run out of salt, a year of disappointments and sorrow will ensue.

Salt must never be loaned to anyone or a quarrel will ensue. However, if someone is so unfortunate as to run out of salt, it may be freely given with no harm done.

Another multi-cultural staple product is bread, and burned bread is a portent of future hunger, job loss, or a bad harvest. Of course, the impact of this omen is less if only part of the loaf is burned. The burned portion should be cut away and buried before the loaf is brought to the table. If the burned bread is discovered after the family is already sitting down to eat, the entire loaf must be buried in the nearest cemetery and salt water tossed over it to ground its curse.

The old expression "to break bread together" is often heard, but few think about its meaning. In old Europe, it was a sign of good faith between two clans or factions to begin a meal with breaking the bread by having two representatives, one from each clan, take hold of the loaf at either end, and tear it in two. At no communal mountain gathering would anyone even think of taking a single bite until the bread is formally broken in this manner.

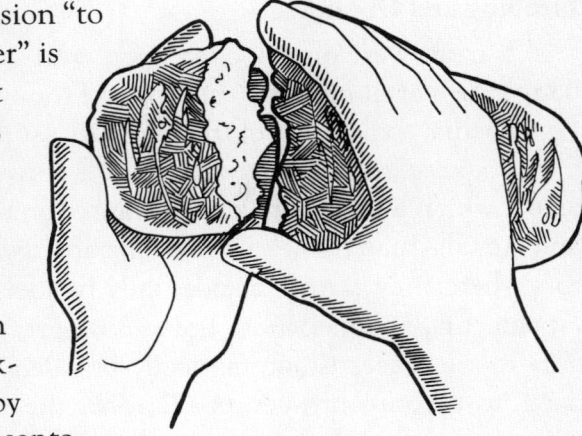

Even within the family, the first helping taken from a serving of *cornbread* must always be "broken" by hand and never cut. Cutting the bread will bring hunger to the house.

An itchy nose at the dinner table means that someone in the family is going to get into a fist fight; an itchy ear means important news is on its way.

Spilling milk means that an evil influence has settled over the home and that steps to break the curse should be taken immediately. Dropping an entire plate of food will bring everyone in the household seven months of bad luck.

As in much of the American South, black-eyed peas must be served on New Year's Day to ensure a bountiful year ahead. Eggs must be eaten on Easter morning, and some people still adhere to the old Pagan belief that they must be eaten on May morning (May 1), a time when they were eaten in honor of the fruitful union of the God and Goddess. An apple eaten on the eve of the autumn equinox will keep you healthy all winter long.

Sleeping and Dreaming

Mirrors were once looked upon with suspicion, viewed as a dangerous portal between the world of form and that of spirit. In Appalachia, some sense of that old mistrust is still in evidence.

Looking into a mirror after dark is considered very bad luck, an act which might even draw unwanted ghosts into the dwelling, and Appalachian homes are carefully arranged to position all mirrors where they cannot accidentally be looked into at night. In Appalachia, anyone whose home is observed to have mirrors in easy-to-see places is automatically branded a witch. This belief dates to seventeenth-century Europe, the first time in history when it was feasible to mass-produce good quality mirrors at an affordable price. In the altered state of consciousness which is a natural part of the sleep cycle, known scientifically as hypnogogic sleep, the mind is very receptive to psychic phenomena. A person who looks into a mirror while in this state will likely see something which is—at best—unexpectedly looking back.

For centuries, magickal folk have deliberately induced these receptive states of mind and used reflective surfaces like mirrors to peer into in hope of seeing visions of the future. This practice is popularly known as scrying. Armed with this magickal knowledge, you may want to arrange your mirrors so that you *can* see into them when walking in the night, rather than avoiding them. Before you go to sleep, fix in your mind one question or issue to which you wish to know the answer or want to more fully understand. This issue has no limits other than your own imagination. You might want to see into a past life, peer at your future, call spirits, view remote events as they happen, or simply ask to see the face of someone dear to you who is far away. If you awaken in the darkness, allow your gaze to remain soft and slightly unfocused as you look into the waiting mirror while you slowly come to consciousness. In this half-sleep state it will take very little practice to see whatever you want to see reflected back at you.

Nightmares can be a sign that you are under a curse. Consuming a large quantity of rye bread laced with your own urine(*) just be-fore going to bed will allow you to dream of the one who has cursed you. If in the dream you see that person from a distance, it means you will not be able to overcome the curse alone. However, if you come face to face with the curser, you have a fighting chance against his magick.

A dream in which you are being ridden means you have had a curse placed on you by a skilled witch who is of the opposite sex from yourself. In medieval England, this was known as being "hag-ridden" and was used as evidence in the courts that the rider was practicing witchcraft, using spells of a sexual nature.

A dream in which you are falling indicates that the spirits have taken your soul for a night trip. This is similar to the belief in astral projection, the deliberate or unconscious expelling of a portion of your soul-self or astral body at night. Many people today believe that a dream about falling occurs when that astral body is returning too rapidly to its physical shell.

Dreaming of blood three nights in a row heralds a war or family feud, and dreaming of thirst forecasts a flood. Night sweats, which can indicate the presence of certain medical conditions such as diabetes, may foretell of a fire.

A sleepwalker is said to be seeking the name of the one who has cursed him, but if someone speaks in their sleep, he is believed to be conversing with spirits, and should not be awakened lest the spirits follow him into the awakened world. If the spectral conversation can be accurately remembered in the morning by the dreamer, any curse from the spirit world is broken.

The sweet-scented herb woodruff is used liberally in mountain homes as a household deodorant, and it has occasionally been stuffed in pillows to bring sweet dreams. You can make one of these dream pillows for yourself by taking a small square of white linen and sewing it up on three sides. Stuff the interior with the woodruff, and sew up the opposite end. You may decorate it with lace or ribbons if you want to and are skilled enough with a needle. Keep this under your regular pillow each night to enhance your dream life and chase away nightmares.

You can also induce dreams of the future by taking a bath in ice water before going to bed, or by having three lit candles burning in your room near your head. If you choose to experiment with the candles, please be aware of the extreme fire hazard!

Eating broad beans, sharp cheeses, or moonshine brewed in an enemy's still—just before bed—can bring on nightmares. However, eating raw eggs, or drinking raw milk or your own home brew can produce entertaining night spectacles. Raw does not mean unpasteurized, just unprocessed. Consuming the unpasteurized product puts you at risk of illness, particularly of contracting salmonella poisoning.

Removing Curses From Home and Person

Appalachian curses come in two varieties: the real and the imagined, though both are equally effective upon the victim. Real curses consist of focused, malevolent energy which has been deliberately and directly sent to you by someone else. Imagined curses are the belief that a real curse has been placed, even when it has not. Human nature being what it is, the mere suggestion of a curse is enough to make it manifest in suggestible individuals. Many would-be witches have used this knowledge to their advantage to strengthen their reputations.

While there are some things a person can do to remove a suspected curse, in Appalachia this is usually the sole province of witches, and their practices are closely guarded secrets. However, there are a few remedies which have been recorded for us in mountain folklore.

To remove a curse from your home, you can try shooting your shotgun out an open window at the full moon, while shouting a curse at the Devil. However, don't try this if you live in a city or populated area, or you will likely find the police at your door.

A simpler method to break a curse on your home is to gather a handful of stones and take them to your fireplace. If you can toss even one clear up through the chimney, the curse is broken.

Or you can purge your home with an incense[5] smoke made from a combination of dried valerian root, dried basil, and rue. The smell is less than pleasant, but it seems to do the job. Move through your home with the incense, making sure every corner and closet is covered, and chant a simple charm such as:

> *Smoke doth fill every living space,*
> *Pushing the bane away from this place.*

In some Appalachian homes, it is traditional to have the eldest member of the household carry the purging incense, while being followed by the youngest, who carries a single lit candle. The glowing candle is symbolic of the new light of hope which is replacing the banished evil, of the light of truth piercing the darkness of deceit, illuminating the unseen, and overcoming fears.

One of the more curious mountain magickal protection devices consists of placing eggshells on a tree. It was once believed that making and having one of these egg trees on your property would drive a curse from your land. In two of my previous books I suggested this practice as a decorative item only, albeit one rife with the Pagan symbolism of new life and fertility.[6] When I came across a couple of references to these trees as Appalachian protective amulets, I became very excited, sure I was about to uncover some forgotten bit of Anglo-Celtic magickal lore which had been lost over the centuries. Unfortunately, I have been unable to trace the origins of the practice, one which has apparently died out in the mountains, except as a decorative item at Easter, nor can anyone explain how the ancient imagery of fertility came to be one of protection.[7]

To make an egg tree, you will need to keep all the shells from the eggs you use for cooking, etc. Instead of cracking them open, with a fork tine or darning needle make a small hole in one end just large enough for you to blow the yolk and whites out into a bowl. This should leave the shell intact. Once you have accumulated a

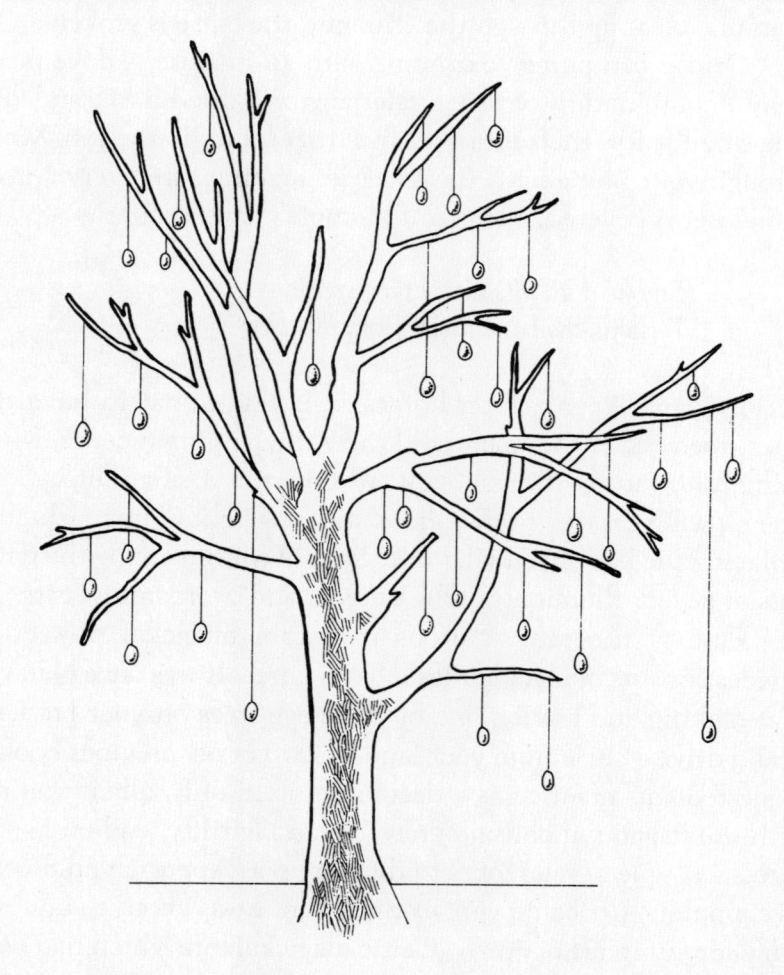

The Egg Tree

collection of shells, make ties for them out of string and tie them onto the branches of a small tree in your yard. The shells will work their magick fine just as they are, but you may feel free to decorate them with paints, dyes, markers, ribbons, etc. Be aware that if it is not spring, your neighbors will find this quirky at best. To avoid their speculation, you may want to bring a branch inside and set it up in a planter and decorate it there.

If you feel an object you own is cursed, then you should give it away. The curse cannot be transferred to another person and, when the curse flees, the object can be given back to you with no harm done. However, if the object is cursed a second time, it is best to burn or bury the item.

To remove a curse from yourself requires a midnight trip or two to your local graveyard. Sleeping there overnight on top of a newly dug grave will remove any curse. Calling out to the spirits of the dead to make themselves visible is another method, probably an act devised to scare the curse out.

Breaking a death curse is a serious matter, one which can be remedied by gathering toxic pokeberries at dusk and taking them to the cemetery just as the sun is setting. Make the full round of the graveyard, placing one berry on each grave to which you come, while chanting a charm such as:

> *Cursed be the one who threw*
> *A curse to turn me into you.*

The word "threw" in this charm is mountain slang. In Appalachia, one is usually said to "throw" rather than cast a curse or spell. When you are finished, the curse will not only be broken, but will have been deflected back to the curser.

If you can magickally call up the shadow of the person who has cursed you, he or she will be forced to remove the curse (though just who forces this is unclear!). To do this, you must go to the graveyard at midnight and pull some grass from around the oldest grave there. On the way home you must see no one, and no one must see you. Once at home, maintain complete silence as you cut a small lock of your hair to mix with the grass. Tie the mixture up in a dark cloth or handkerchief, then toss the bundle out the window. The shade of the one who has cursed you should appear standing just outside. When he does, you must not show any fear or surprise, but instead laugh out loud at the apparition. The image should fade and the curse be gone by daybreak.

The Magick in Household Tasks

The old European view of housework as a magickal act still abounds in Appalachia. This link is evident in the language we still use when discussing the making of magick as "casting a spell" (from knitting), "brewing a spell" (from cooking), "spinning a spell" (from spinning thread), or "weaving magick" (from weaving cloth).

Spinning—In Europe, spinning was a very magickal act because of its symbolic connection to the myths of the spinning virgin Goddesses, who created all things from their wheels. In Appalachia, some of these magical connotations still exist, even though their original meanings have been largely forgotten. The task of spinning is always given to the eldest daughter, until her wedding day. If she never marries she becomes a "spinster," a label still widely used in the English language when referring to an older, single woman. A young woman would often dream of her future husband while spinning in the hope that she would magically draw that mate into her life.

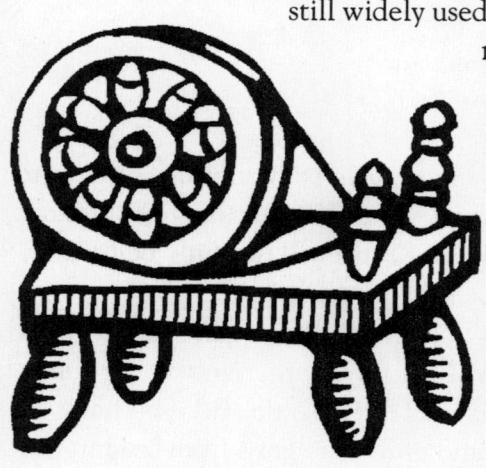

Singing—One of the most prevalent magickal housetask beliefs is still found in the practice of singing or chanting to speed the work process, a concept which comes directly from the folklore of the Scottish Highlands where many working songs have been preserved and recorded by musicologists. Singing while working was likely first done to help pass the time, but it soon developed its own magickal connotations. For example, chanting always must be done while churning in Appalachia, in order to "bring" the butter. Failure to do so simply means that you can churn all day and all night and get nothing but beaten milk.

In Appalachia, singing is almost a requirement when spinning. Many of the traditional spinning songs employ a variety of nonsense syllables which mean nothing in and of themselves (see the music to *Sarasponda* in this chapter), but act as a focal point for lulling the mind into a receptive state, one perfect for focusing on magickal intents while working. This is done by allowing the mind to project the need outward while the rhythm of the wheel lulls the mind. To make the music more in tune with the rising magickal energies, each succeeding verse is usually sung one half-step higher than the one it follows. The energies raised while spinning can be directed to almost any need. Common spinning

Sarasponda
(An Appalachian Spinning Song)

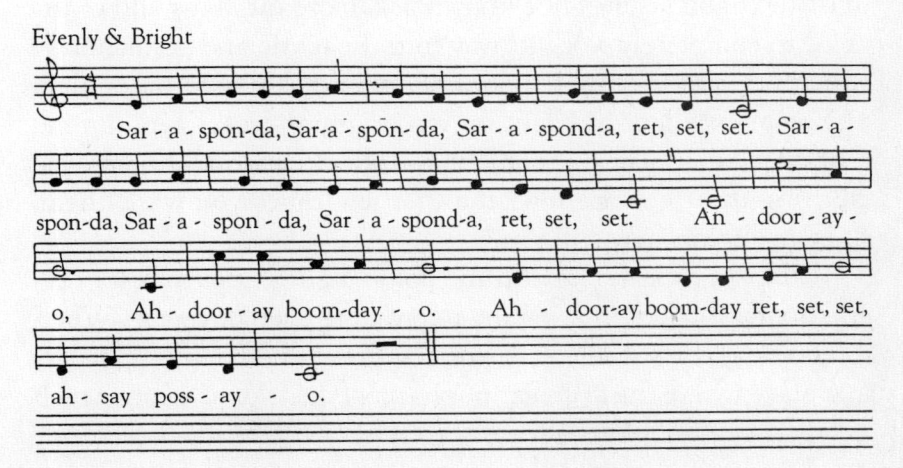

Evenly & Bright

Sar-a-spon-da, Sar-a-spon-da, Sar-a-spond-a, ret, set, set. Sar-a-spon-da, Sar-a-spon-da, Sar-a-spond-a, ret, set, set. An-door-ay-o, Ah-door-ay boom-day-o. Ah-door-ay boom-day ret, set, set, ah-say poss-ay-o.

magick in Appalachia is used to raise a cohesive protective barrier around the home, send healing energy to a sick loved one, to bring love, or to turn evil away from someone who is cursed.

Weaving and Dying—Weaving spun fibers into cloth, or knitting with yarn made at the wheel, also have magickal associations. Again, singing with the rhythm of the loom or the clacking of the knitting needles promotes a magical state of consciousness which can be used for a variety of purposes.

Whether homemade or store-bought, cloth can be infused with magickal intent, but in the mountains, the patterns woven into the clothing have far less impact than the colors chosen. Even if you cannot weave your own fabric, or have no interest in doing so, you can still use natural materials to dye light-colored or unbleached fabric. Just the fact that you are going through this process will help infuse the act with a strong magical intent.

To home-dye unbleached cloth or yarn, begin with a large iron pot (other metals will take the dye permanently and should not be used), toss in a generous amount of the crushed herbs, and allow them to simmer over a very low heat. The final dye color will be several shades lighter than the water color, so you may wish to add extra herbs if you desire a darker shade.

When you think you have the right color in the water, you must next add a substance known as a mordant. This allows the color to completely work its way into the fabric and permanently adhere. A couple of tablespoons of either cream of tartar or alum makes an excellent mordant for most natural dyes. Keep in mind that even when using a mordant you should wash all home-dyed clothing in a separate load the first few times you wash them, since the colors may still run.

Place the clean fabric in the pot and allow it to soak for several hours, stirring occasionally to promote even coverage. When the fabric is the shade you desire, remove it and hang it up to dry in a place where the drips cannot harm or discolor anything (such as on an outdoor clothesline).

Natural fabric dyes don't come only from the Appalachian woodlands. You can easily grow or order these plants for your own use (see Appendix A). The following is a list of magical color symbolisms in Appalachia, many of which have similar associations in western Europe, and the plants which will produce them:

Color	Source(s)	Magickal Meaning(s)
Red	Madder, Red Onion Skins	Passion, Lust, Strength
Pink	Heather, Wild Ginger Root	Romance, Peace
Orange	Aster, Onion Skins, Goldenrod, Carrot Tops, Bracken Root	Health, Labor, Law
Yellow	Black Hickory Bark, Turmeric Root, Ragwort, White Grapes	Intellect, Communication
Green	Oak Leaves, Coltsfoot Leaves, Elder Leaves, Bracken Stems	Fertility, Prosperity, Luck, Agriculture
Blue	Red Cabbage, Bearberry Root, Indigo, Black Raspberries	Spirituality, Fidelity, Dream Work
Violet	Pokeberry Root, Elder Berries, Mullberries, Blueberries	Healing, Clairvoyance, Astral Projection
Brown	Walnut Hulls, Pine Cones, Pine Tar, Red Root	Earth, Home, Animals
Black	Black Walnuts, Bramble	Absorption, The Hidden

Cooking—Cooking has also been used as a magickal activity; in fact, there is an entire genre of magick known as "Kitchen Witchery" which is very popular in Appalachia.

Molding breads into certain shapes and consuming them to make them a part of one's life is ancient magick indeed. For instance, if you need love in your life, bake a loaf in the shape of a heart; or if you need a job, make the loaf look like a $20 bill! As you consume the bread, you bring into yourself that which you desire.

Potpourris—Setting aromatic herbs on the stove to boil and impart their fragrance to the room for magickal purposes is common household magick, even today. (The energy-conscious Witch may want to look in craft shops for small ceramic double-boilers which use tea candles to heat the herbs.) For example, rosemary and cloves tossed in together make a delightful scent, one which also has exorcism capabilities. However, keep in mind that scent has almost nothing to do with the magickal effectiveness of a substance, and some of the best herbs for cooking magick smell less than terrific when boiling.

Begin experimenting with boiling potpourris by referring to the following list of common, non-toxic Appalachian herbs/fruits and their magickal properties. Feel free to mix blends to suit your needs and your nose:

Herb	Magickal Properties
Apple Blossom	Romance, Love
Apple Cores, Dried	Healing
Asafetida	Purification, Protection
Basil	Protection, Fidelity
Bay Laurel	Exorcism
Bistort	Fertility
Cinnamon	Protection, Exorcism
Clove	Protection, Binding
Ferns	Fertility
Honeysuckle	Prosperity
Ginger	Prosperity, Luck
Goldenseal	Healing, Prosperity
Linden Flowers	Protection, Dream Magick
Magnolia	Fidelity, Peace
Mint	Protection, Healing
Myrtle	Love, Fertility
Peaches, Dried	Happiness, Fertility
Pears, Dried	Love
Pennyroyal	Vigor, Protection
Persimmons, Dried	Healing
Pine Cones	Prosperity, Fertility
Pumpkin, Dried	Healing, Clairvoyance
Rosemary	Protection, Intellect, Love
Rue	Fidelity, Unity
Sage, Wild	Intellect, Protection
Sassafras Bark	Prosperity, Healing
Valerian Root	Astral Projection, Psychic Work

Gardening and Farming "By the Signs"

One of the old ways which shows absolutely no sign of dying out in Appalachia is that of planting, harvesting, and farming by using astrological phenomena as a guide. Whether the moon is new or old, and which sign it is traversing are the two primary criteria for making horticultural decisions.[9]

In Appalachia, the terms used to describe these transits differ from those most often heard to describe aspects of moon astrology. Mountain people divide the moon's cycle into only two phases: the new (from new to full) and old (from full to dark). They also tend to discuss the twelve astrological signs in terms of the parts of the body they rule. Up in the mountains it is not unusual to hear a gardener talking about waiting to do the weeding "until the moon is in the heart," referring to the sign of Leo which governs that organ. Weeding is done at this time because Leo is a fire sign and, unlike the watery signs, fire is barren. Tasks begun during this transit yield little. In other words, the weeds will grow back more slowly.

In general, water signs within a new moon are the choice times for planting those things which you want to flourish—particularly true when the moon is in the stomach (Cancer).

Sign	Element	Associated Body Parts
Aries	Fire	Head and Face
Taurus	Earth	Neck and Throat
Gemini	Air	Hands, Arms, Shoulders, Lungs
Cancer	Water	Stomach, Breasts, Solar Plexus
Leo	Fire	Back, Heart, Liver
Virgo	Earth	Intestines, Nerves, Pancreas
Libra	Air	Lumbar Region, Kidneys, Buttocks
Scorpio	Water	Genitals and Bladder
Sagittarius	Fire	Hips and Thighs
Capricorn	Earth	Bones, Joints, Knees, Ligaments
Aquarius	Air	Vascular System, Legs, Ankles
Pisces	Water	Feet and Toes

Any beans planted on a new moon will rot. Beans should be planted on Good Friday unless the moon is in the head (Aries).

Potatoes planted on a new moon will grow large but sparse. They are best planted in the feet (Pisces).

All greens should be planted on the old moon in an earth sign.

Plant nothing in the intestines (Virgo), and avoid the heart (Leo) and the head (Aries) whenever possible.

Cucumbers and beans both grow best when planted in the arms (Gemini).

Plant lettuce and cabbage on the new moon in March, and onions on an old moon in April.

Peas give the best yield when planted in the genitals (Scorpio), and turnips when planted in the legs (Aquarius).

Cabbage should go in on the Fourth of July unless the moon is in the heart (Leo).

No plant should ever be transplanted when the moon is in the heart (Leo) or head (Aries).

Plant carrots, beets, and sweet potatoes when the moon is in the bones (Capricorn).

Apples and pears should always be picked on an old moon.

Corn planted in the heart (Leo) will become diseased. Corn is best planted on a new moon after May 1 or when the oak leaves are one full week into their spring budding.

In Pagan Europe, August 1 was known as Lammas (meaning "loaf mass"), the celebration of the grain harvest and of the loaves of bread (a staple food) the harvest would yield. Memories of this tradition are evoked each year in the mountain people's timing for their own corn harvest. Many old timers insist that when the cicadas—insects of the aphid family which make a locust-like buzzing to attract mates—start calling, it is time to harvest the corn. They also insist that this will *always* take place on or near August 1.

There is a prevalent taboo against picking and eating wild berries of any kind after the end of September. This is another of the old Celtic beliefs, one which has roots in the worship of Pagan deities to whom berries were sacred. Most notably taboo are wild blackberries, which were sacred to Brighid in Ireland and to Thor in Scandinavia. The only exception to this taboo was if the berries were made into a wine dedicated in honor of the deity, another concept adopted in Appalachia where recipes for delicate berry wines remain closely guarded family secrets.

Because squash and other gourds are harvested late in autumn, they are deeply linked in the mountain mind with death. Again, this has to do with beliefs the Celts had about the seasons. Autumn was a time of slowing, preparing for the long winter repose after the hectic activity of summer. It was a time when the old Gods slept or died, just like the landscape, and, to the mountain folk, items connected with this dying time were intimately linked together. Because squash are edible and grow well in the mountain climate, they are still widely harvested, but they are often looked at with a tad of suspicion and are never brought into homes to serve as seasonal decorations, as they sometimes are in other parts of the country. Mountain folks say the gardeners who grow the best squash are those who are "not quite all there in the head."

Omens from the Land and Its Folk

Cutting broom straws which will be used to make a household broom is bad luck after dark. Clearing a field on a dark moon is also a bad practice, one which could invite negative influences to settle there.

If you find yourself in a place where you see a four-petaled wakerobin, a red or white wildflower which normally has only three petals, back quickly away, for you are in an accursed place.

A dead mayflower plant, one which blossoms with a leathery pink or white flower in the spring, abundant in the mountains, is a disastrous omen, since the plant is known to be perennial.

Certain caves in the remote hills have a reputation for being "caves of no return," and are to be scrupulously avoided. These caves are ones into which people have ventured, but from which they never emerge. Many legends have been told about these caves, most involving the spirit world, but it is more likely that the hapless spelunker came across people engaged in illegal activities such as blockading, and met with foul play.

Bright lights seen in the night sky, such as the Aurora Borealis, foretell of events of great import. Mountain folks say that the American Civil War, until recent times always referred to as the War Between the States, was heralded by a light show in the sky.

You should always make a wish on the first fruits or berries of the season. It may not come true, but not to try is an insult to the spirit of the land on which it grows, and the slight may cause blighted crops in the year to come.

The mountain people also have omens connected with themselves, many of which have fallen out of favor over the past few decades. For instance, a hairy man is considered to be exceptionally virile, a hairy woman a powerful witch. A man with a thick beard is destined to be a great leader, and one with a long beard displays a sign of wisdom. A woman whose hair went gray young was likely to discover she had witch powers, and early balding in men was a similar indication.

Hair from the heads of family members is often shorn and laid upon newly dug graves as an offering to the ancestors, a Pagan custom from both central Europe and the Middle East. This is not only a sign of respect to the dead, but one which binds the lives of the family to the spirits of their collective past. The ancestors will then be obligated to patrol the graveyard for their descendants, keeping at bay any ghostly presences which might seek to harm them.

Protruding nasal hairs indicate a pious soul, and protruding ear hairs are a sign of laziness.

A long-fingered person is supposed to be a skilled hunter, and a short-fingered one a good weaver. Someone with long fingernails is thought to be skilled with his or her hands in artistic or mechanical matters.

Eyes which are set close together are not only a sign of low intellect, but also mean that the person has been gifted with second sight. Wide-set eyes indicate a shifty character who is not to be trusted.

Large hands are a sign of a generous soul, but large feet forecast a life of poverty.

A wart on a ring finger means poor marriage prospects, but one on the neck indicates the birth of many healthy children. Warts on the feet belie a steadfast and loyal nature, but on the hands they foretell a life of hard work ahead.

Webbing between the toes is another sign of a person with special magickal powers, but webbing between the hands suggests someone gifted with animals, crops, or healing.

Bushy eyebrows signify a distrustful nature, while crooked ears are a sign of a trusting fool.

Large ears are the mark of a skilled and enduring lover, small ears a sign of infertility.

Eyes which are of two different colors mean one has the gift of clairvoyance and the ability to see spirits.

In keeping with a very ancient tradition, the seventh daughter of a seventh daughter, or the seventh son of a seventh son, possesses strong magickal powers which need only to be developed.

Omens and Magick of Animals

Hunting and fishing have always been more than mere sport to the mountain folk—they are a means for putting food on the table of a hungry family. As with gardening and farming, if a mountaineer wished to have the greatest possible success in his endeavors, he would follow certain omens and guidelines.[10]

Animals hunted for food should not be killed on a new moon or the meat will rot.

Hunting knives and guns must never be given, but must be bought by the hunter, or the gift earned through some effort on the part of the recipient.

When the moon is in the throat (Taurus) is the best time to hunt, but the fishing is best when the moon is in the feet (Pisces).

A wild hog will not attack a hunter who carries a pocketful of blue or amber beads.

Bears and predatory cats are most active when the moon is in the heart (Leo), but wolves prefer the moon in the stomach (Cancer).

A deer shot by an arrow rather than a rifle makes healthier meat which is slower to spoil.

Look for possum to be most active on the old moon.

You will be most successful hunting squirrel when the moon is in the kidneys (Libra).

Rabbits like to forage under the full moon and are most active at dusk and dawn. They are also attracted to meadow-like areas where birch trees grow.

Turkey should never be hunted when the moon is new or in the thighs (Sagittarius).

A raccoon pelt on the wall of your home will bring good luck to those who live there.

To keep your favorite hunting dog from running away, you must cut a stick the exact length of his tail and bury it near your home with some of his feces.

Fish for pleasure any time, but if you need food for your table you should fish when the moon is in a water sign or in the ankles (Aquarius). Use cheese for bait to catch the biggest fish, and carry a blue stone in your left pocket for the tastiest catch.

The appearance, color, and condition of wild and domestic animals can tell the observant mountaineer much about his future, just as they did for his Celtic ancestors. Many of these animals have been discussed in previous chapters where they pertain to death, illness, etc., but a host of other miscellaneous signs are known in Appalachia.

The most benevolent—almost sacred—of Appalachian animals is the bee. Their presence indicates good fortune for those on whose land they live. They will only sting someone who is dirty or wicked, but they will make honey for and look after the pure of heart. Skilled beekeepers abound in the mountains, and their reputation is legendary. Almost everyone wants bees around, if for no other reason than to show off, and so this talent is cultivated.

Bees become very attached to the keeper and their keeper's family even though they are kept in beegums, hollow tubes of trunk from a black gum tree, and not in the home. Bees must always be given the courtesy of being told of family deaths or they will leave or die, and, naturally, terrible luck ensues with their departure. In the case of the death of their keeper, there are numerous documented cases where the hive has attended the funeral, then moved on to a new home.[11]

If you want to have bees around your place, either plant lots of the herb known as lemon balm, or start a garden of flowering plants. Both will draw and keep the attention of bees.

Spiders are also friendly creatures, seen by some as servants of God. The symbolism of the spider as a messenger of God may harken back to many of the old Pagan creation myths which feature spider-like Goddesses spinning all things into creation. To have spider webs about you is considered a blessing in Appalachia, a sign of good fortune to come and an indication of God's favor. Waking up at dawn to see a newly spun web is a sign of exceptionally good luck. If it is across a door, the web must not be broken until sunrise the next day.

As has already been noted, owls are omens of great ill. If you spot one nearby while you are inside your home, the direction in which it flies away is an indication of the fate of your household. If it flies off to the left of the cabin, very bad luck can be expected, but if it flies off to the right, it indicates an evil influence has chosen to pass you by. Though most folks would probably consider being hit by bird droppings most unfortunate, many Appalachian folk believe this brings blessings from heaven.

Snakes, even the non-poisonous variety, are not viewed favorably as a direct result of the Genesis creation myth in which a serpent tempted Adam and Eve into committing the transgressions which ultimately got them expelled from their garden paradise. Young children and domestic animals are particularly susceptible to the wiles of the snake, and many mountain legends abound about children who keep them as secret pets and do their bidding, or of cows who allow them to feed from their udders.[12]

Cats abroad in the night are a sign that some mischief of a spectral nature is lurking about. They are also believed, as they were in old Europe, to be the working partners, or familiars, of witches. Though their presence may not be welcome, they are never harassed, for fear of offending a local witch.

Mice are also viewed as bad omens, likely because of their association with disease. The weasel, a close cousin of the mouse, is also an unwelcome visitor, and is usually shot on sight.

When seen at night, hares, usually considered as either servants of the Devil or as disguised demons, are portents of very bad times ahead. Seen during the daylight hours, they mean nothing but a free meal to a skilled hunter.

Possums are good luck, a sign of coming abundance, especially if one is spotted with her young.

A goose who lays her first egg of the year on March 17 will bring great fortune to her owner.

Cows must be kept in odd numbers or risk the entire herd falling ill.

Swine are probably the most widely kept feed animals in the mountains, and they are considered very lucky to have around. You must never allow anyone to pull a pig's tail, though, or all the luck will vanish and his meat will go bad.

A frog which finds its way into your home brings good luck, one which finds you in the wild means you should be cautious until you return safely home.

Toads are usually killed if they come into a home, for it is believed that they are serving the will of a local witch. When discovered out in the wild they are omens of good luck.

Endnotes to Chapter 5

1. Wigginton, Eliot, ed. *The Foxfire Book* (Garden City, NY: Doubleday and Co., 1972), Chapter Two.

2. Cole, Joanna, ed. *Best-Loved Folktales of the World* (Garden City, NY: Doubleday and Company, Inc., 1982).

3. McCoy, Edain. *A Witch's Guide to Faery Folk* (St. Paul, MN: Llewellyn Worldwide, 1994), pp. 72-73.

4. For an example of adapting this spell to the beliefs of another magickal tradition, please see Chapter Eight.

5. An excellent guide to making and using your own magickal incenses is Scott Cunningham's *The Complete Book of Incense, Oils and Brews* (Llewellyn, 1989).

6. *Witta: An Irish Pagan Tradition* and *The Sabbats: A New Approach to Living the Old Ways* (both Llewellyn).

7. In my search, I was directed to a book on Ozark Mountain folklore and discovered a similar practice, but still no hint at either its place or era of origin, or how it came to be a protective image rather than one of fertility. The practice probably traveled to the Ozarks with migrating Appalachian people, as the two regions share startlingly similar magickal beliefs.

9. For those interested in learning and/or following the movements of the moon and zodiac, I heartily recommend either the *Moon Sign Book* or *Daily Planetary Guide*, both published annually by Llewellyn Worldwide.

10. For more on Appalachian hunting lore, particularly tall tales from the region, see either *The Foxfire Book*, *Foxfire 5* (both Doubleday and Co., 1972 and 1986), or Hodge C. Mathes' *Tall Tales From Old Smokey* (Southern Publishers, Inc., 1952).

11. Reynolds, George P. and students, eds. *Foxfire 9* (New York: Doubleday and Co., 1986). You may also want to look into any of the books on the psychic abilities of animals currently on the market which contain similar stories.

12. *The Foxfire Book* (Doubleday and Co., 1972) has an entire chapter devoted to snake lore.

CHAPTER SIX

Love, Marriage, and Fidelity

I wish I had a needle
As fine as I could sew,
I'd sew my true love to my side
and down the road we'd go.
 —Traditional Mountain Dancing Song

When studying the folk magick of any culture—past or present—one thing quickly becomes evident: more than any other type of spell or omen, those concerning love and marriage seem to be most prevalent. They are not always practical or easy to implement, and they are certainly the most prone to ethical abuses, but they nonetheless abound, and are often turned to when all else fails, even by the most hardened Doubting Thomas.

Old Maids and Love Divinations

In spite of the fact that spinsters, and sometimes even widows, have been regarded as the most powerful witches and granny women in the mountains, it has still been believed better to be married. The worst fate which the Appalachian people felt could befall a young woman was that of being "left an old maid," or of remaining unmarried all her life. Life was hard in the mountains, and young people needed strong partners to help them survive. To this end, mountain folks married very young. Teens who were not wed by sixteen were considered slow bloomers, and those not married by eighteen were thought to be lost causes. Anyone who has ever seen the television sitcom, "The Beverly Hillbillies," will probably remember Granny trying to convince potential suitors that her womanly granddaughter, Ellie Mae, was a very marriageable fourteen years old!

Naturally, there are omens to watch for, taboos to observe, and many divinations to help you discover if you, or your daughter, will remain unwed.

Caution must always be taken when sweeping the floors around an unmarried girl so that the broom does not accidentally brush over her feet, or she will be doomed to remain an old maid. I first heard this omen from a first generation African woman, so it is conceivable that the belief may have come into Appalachian folklore through contact with slaves. Since the popular Pagan wedding custom of "jumping [over] the broom[stick]" originated in Africa—rather than Europe as many believe—this omen may have been based on a backward visual concept that the broom was jumping the girl, thus negating her chances of ever jumping over it.

Dropping a comb while combing one's hair in the evening is also indicative of spinsterhood. In both cases, the curse can be lessened by burying or burning the offending object in the local cemetery or at an isolated crossroad. Combing the hair between sunset and sunrise will comb a man out of a young lady's future.

No single woman is ever permitted to put the last stitch in a quilt, for this would fate her to live single forever.

Coming across a lone wolf in the woods is another sign of spinsterhood, possibly because the wolf is known to mate for life and to rarely be far from its partner. To see one alone is a portent of a life of loneliness.

Another creature which mates for life is the bird. Single persons who wish to marry within the year should keep an eye out for the coming of the first spring birds. If they appear in pairs, you will be part of a couple before the next coming of spring, but if you see the birds come one by one, you too will end the year single.

While it seems a lesser concern whether or not Appalachian males marry, most do. However, if an unmarried boy nicks himself in the ring finger with his own pocket knife, then it is likely that no woman will have him. Plunging the knife blade into the ground and leaving it overnight can help lessen this curse, though it certainly doesn't do much good for the knife.

For some young people, being pursued by the wrong person can be a worse fate than having no one at all. A girl will either carry poppies to ward off unwanted suitors, or hang dirty linens or headgear up over the front door to drive them away. A boy will rub his hands on a frog before going out where the girl he dreads to meet might be waiting for him.

If you want to catch a glimpse of your future mate, you should take a minister's gardening tool to a graveyard at midnight and plunge it into the earth. Close your eyes and ask the guardian of the cemetery to allow you a glimpse of the shade of your partner-to-be. Then face east and you should see the shadow of your future mate walk past. If he travels from south to north, you will have a happy marriage; from north to south, a passionate one. If he walks from east to west, you will be decidedly unhappy; and from west to east, you will be contented, but poor. If no shadow appears, you either are doomed to a life of spinsterhood, or else you picked up the wrong garden tool.[1]

If you take a handful of violet buds and toss them haphazardly in front of you while thinking thoughts of romance, they will fall into a pattern which suggests the name or initials of your future mate. If this divination works best for you with purple violet blossoms, your marriage will be a passionate one; if white blossoms work best, your mate will always be faithful.

A young woman can see her future love reflected in a mirror if she sits before it just before sundown and combs her hair down over her face. Brush slowly for one hundred strokes, then peer through the veil of hair into the mirror. Be warned that you should never allow this ritual to proceed into the hours of darkness or the reflection seen will be a vision of your own funeral.

An Appalachian girl who reaches puberty will often be given a traditional "quilting," a gathering where the women of the community make a special quilt for her to place in her hope chest.[2] This practice harkens back to the Celtic past when young women and young men were honored in the community as spiritual adults upon reaching certain age/physical milestones, and gifted with items which they could use as adults. Even the quilt itself has magickal abilities. It contains, sewn up in its fibers, the good wishes of all who worked on it, and since intent is nine-tenths of magick, it is a powerful gift indeed. The cover is also symbolic of the future home which the girl will share with the man she loves, and therefore acts as a magickal magnet to help draw him to her. The girl for whom the quilt is made is not supposed to sleep under it until her wedding night, but most mountain girls know that if they can sneak it onto their beds, and sleep under it just for one night, that they will dream of their future mate.

From Pagan Europe comes the well-known custom of placing a sliver of wedding cake under your pillow to inspire a dream of your destined partner, a practice which is also observed in Appalachia. If you kiss the cake before going to bed you will dream of your actual wedding day.

Love, Marriage, and Fidelity

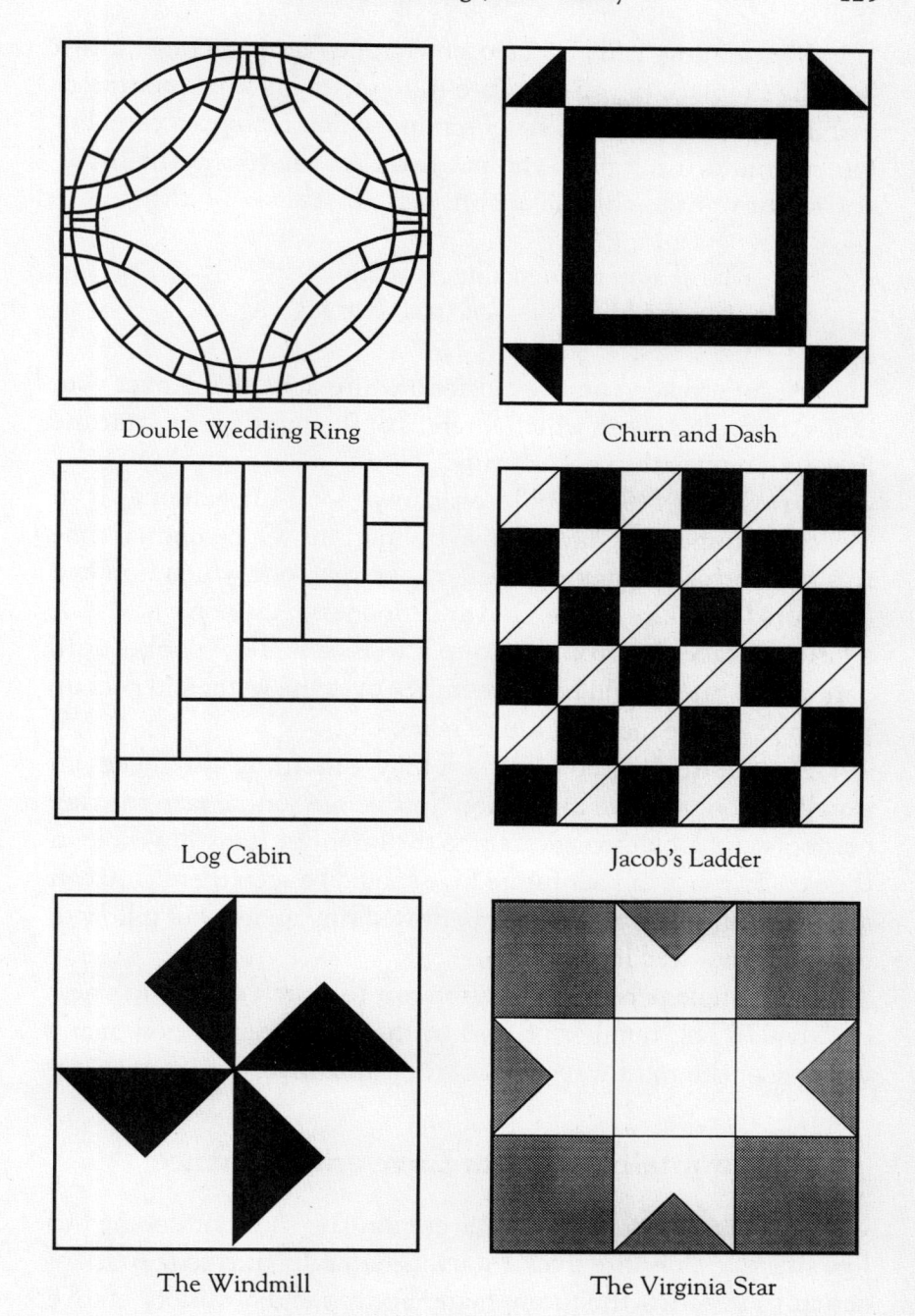

Double Wedding Ring

Churn and Dash

Log Cabin

Jacob's Ladder

The Windmill

The Virginia Star

Common Quilt Patterns

Myrtle sprigs can be tossed slowly, one piece at a time, into a burning fireplace as you gaze into it, to see the face of your future mate. This is the ancient art of scrying which requires a calm but focused mind, a soft gaze, and patience. As you toss in the herbs, you might want to chant a charm such as:

> *Myrtle sweet as a mountain spring,*
> *Show me he (or she) who will wear my ring.*

Be sure to keep an eye out for a white dove flying over your house, a surefire omen which foretells of the marriage of someone in your family within a year's time.

In keeping with the old Celtic ways, May 1 (Bealtaine) is an especially important day for love divinations. Once upon a time this was one of the major festivals of the year, one which honored the sacred marriage of the God and Goddess. At noon on May 1, a girl may take a mirror and go to a well or shallow pool of still, dark water. She should hold the mirror over the water and peer up into it to see the face of a future mate.

A wedding ring borrowed on May 1 morning also makes an excellent tool for love divination. Just before sunup, take the ring outdoors and look through it up to the brightest star still visible in the sky. The face of your future love should be seen there. You can also sleep on May eve with the borrowed ring under your pillow to dream of your wedding.

The single person might also want to search out a bird's nest on May 1. The number of eggs in the nest foretells how many years he or she must wait to meet their true love.

Mountain Spells for Love and Romance

Once a young man or woman is certain they are not doomed to live single their entire lives, thoughts naturally turn to the task of actually attracting the future mate. To that end, a variety of love spells are employed.

A Celtic tradition which has been preserved in myths and nursery rhymes, and which is widely known in the mountains, says that if it rains on the eve of May, a smart single person should place a barrel or pot out to catch the water. Bathe with it just as the sun comes up, then go seek out the one you love. Washed in the May water, you will be irresistible.[3] Other spring rainwater can be charged to similar magickal effectiveness by placing nine blossoms from a flowering tree into it, and allowing this to soak overnight. Bathe with it at sunrise while thinking romantic thoughts, then go seek your love.

To draw that special love into your life you might need to resort to one of the oldest spells on earth—a binding spell using homemade poppets or dolls. This is sympathetic magick in its purest form, using like images to draw like results. The poppets can be store-brought, but for magickal purposes they will work much better if they are made by your own hand. For a love spell, you will need two of them, and they need not be fancy. The most important criteria is that you infuse them with your magickal intent.

If you prefer to make poppets from organic material, dried corn husks, corn shocks, or wheat sheaves are the plants which will most easily weave into poppets, and these are readily found in craft shops. Twist these into human forms by making a long torso, a head, and two arms and legs. Use twine or craft wire to tie off and differentiate the areas as you go. Be sure as you work to mentally project the identity of the poppet into the making. One of these will represent you, and the other will be someone you wish to draw into your life. Though it is not in keeping with Appalachian practice, it is recommended that, in order to avoid the repercussions of magickal manipulation, you not project onto the other poppet the identity of someone who is actually known to you. Instead, focus on the qualities of the sort of person you want to have in your life.

You can also make the poppets from cloth (white linen is preferred) even if you are not very handy with a needle. The easiest way to do this is to cut out four identical forms, no more than six to eight inches in height, and then stitch up all sides but one. Use this opening to stuff the interior with a love-drawing herb such as myrtle or rosemary, then sew up the remaining end.

When the poppets are completed, tie them face to face with a red (for passion) or pink (for romance) string and place them under your pillow. You might also want to dress them up with sprigs of myrtle, violet, dogwood or cowslip—all herbs which are heavily used in mountain love magick and divination. Every night before you go to bed, kiss the poppets and, with all the feeling you can muster, utter a charm such as:

(for poppets made of grains)
Bound tonight warm in my bed,
Heart to heart and head to head.
Now out of corn and into flesh,
Switched be they when the grain
   is threshed.

(for poppets sewn and stuffed)
Bound tonight warm in my bed,
Heart to heart and head to head.
Herb which knows the loves of all,
Make him (or her) in love now fall.

Keep up this spell until it is successful, then hide the poppets away where they cannot be discovered. If they are ever unearthed, or the tie binding them is ever removed, the spell will be broken and have to be redone.

If a girl winks at the brightest star in the heavens which she can see from her own bedroom window, she will get the man of her choice. If she speaks his name and tells the star to wish him good-night, he will dream of her.

From East Anglia in England comes this mountain spell to induce your love to come to you. Take three candles (a big

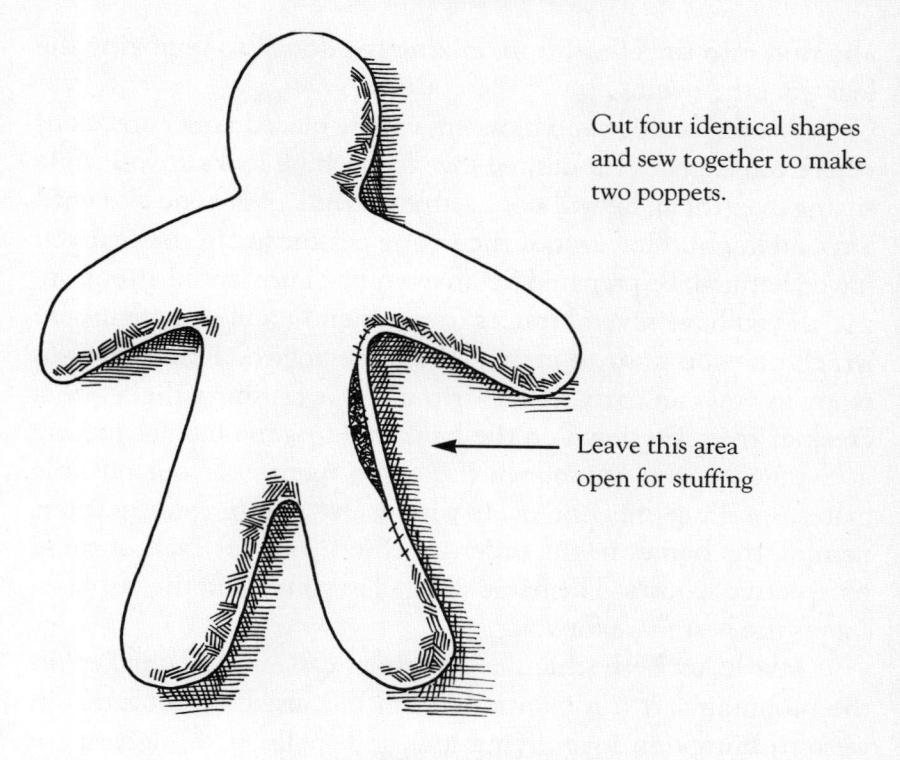

Cut four identical shapes and sew together to make two poppets.

Leave this area open for stuffing

Making a Poppet

expense in the poor mountains!) to a graveyard at dawn, lay them on a bed of wild violets if they are available, or cover them with the blossoms which you have brought with you from another location. Go back to retrieve the candles at midnight and take them home. Set them all burning at once in your bedroom. When you awaken, take the nubs and bury them near your bedroom window with some of the violets which cradled them in the graveyard. As long as these remain undisturbed, the object of your desire will be drawn repeatedly to your home.[4]

Another English spell which found its way to the mountains involves baking a loaf of bread onto which the name of the desired love has been carved prior to baking. When the loaf is shared between the baker and his or her desired mate, an engagement is almost a certainty. Be sure to put lots of feeling and visualization into the effort, from mixing the dough to removing the loaf from the oven.

Cowslip or dogwood blossoms can be placed under any chair where you expect your desired love to sit. If he looks at you while sitting over them, he will not be able to think of anyone else until after midnight. However, if the wrong person sits in the seat you have charmed, be prepared for an evening of unwanted attention.

If you have several suitors or girl friends, and you are unsure which one you want to marry, take some dogwood blossoms—as many as you can carry in one trip without crushing them—to a creek or river. Sit down on the bank and toss the blooms in, one at a time, as you pronounce the given names of your possible mates, speaking only one name with each blossom you toss. Start naming the names in the order in which you met each of these prospective spouses. The name you call as you toss in the last blossom is the best mate for you.

Myrtle, an herb which is sometimes called "matchmaker" in the mountains, is a romantic herb of old, used for centuries in western Europe in love divinations and spells. If, while you are wearing myrtle where it can be seen by all, you are able to touch the flesh of the one you desire, he will instantly fall in love with you. If you can induce him to also wear a sprig of myrtle, you are as good as engaged.

Rue is another popular herb used in mountain love magick, which is how it earned its nickname "bridewort." If you can manage to add just the tiniest bit of it to a drink which your desired love will be sipping, he will fall in love with you—as long as you are the first one he sees after both the first sip and the last sip is taken from the charmed cup. Rue which is powdered and blown from your palm into a wind blowing in the direction of your loved one's home will produce his presence within twenty-four hours.

Rue and rosemary left burning together on a hearth will keep two lovers' families sound asleep and unaware if the couple is seeking a night-time elopement.

Rosemary can also be scattered near a threshold while chanting the name of the one you love. If he or she walks across it to enter your home, his heart will remain there with you.

As you scatter the herb, chant a charm such as:

> Pass the threshold, pass the door,
> Love comes to me when he (she) crosses o'er.
> Tightly bound and never to stray,
> He (She) shall not pass out nor slip away.

Magick and the Mountain Marriage

Appalachian weddings are rife with ancient customs and beliefs. For instance, it is considered very bad luck to marry on a Friday. This belief comes from medieval Europe where it was firmly believed that, since Friday was the day on which Jesus was sacrificed, nothing started on this day could come to any good. Monday, which takes its name from the moon, the planet which governs fertility, is considered the best day for weddings, especially if the couple wants lots of children.

It is not only bad luck, but also in poor taste, to marry twice in the same place regardless of how well the first marriage turned out.

A bride who wishes for happiness should never make her own wedding dress, and a groom who wants a joyous life should never wear old shoes to his marriage.

On the day of the wedding, bread and salt should be taken into the home which the couple will share. These two European staple foods act as talismans of prosperity so that the couple will never be hungry. This custom is probably many thousands of years old, coming to Europe from the Middle East. Even in modern Judaism, bread and salt are still a central part of the official blessing for a new home.

Mountain wedding decorations are traditionally kept simple, and are usually gleaned from the land, a practice still followed in very rural or poor areas. Wildflowers, flowering herbs, and native grain stalks are the items most often chosen, not only because they are handy, but because they possess a magickal symbolism of their own. The following is a brief list of the magickal associations of common wedding foliage from rural Appalachia:[5]

Foliage	Magickal Meaning
Apple Blossom	Romance
Bachelor Buttons	Fidelity
Basil	Protection, Fidelity
Blue Vervain	Love
Bluebells	Protection
Celedine (toxic)	Fidelity, Eternity
Corn Shocks	Abundance
Cranesbill	Good Luck
Dogwood	Love
Ferns	Fertility
Goldenrod	Prosperity
Honeysuckle	Prosperity
Hydrangea (toxic)	Abundance, Romance
Ivy	Fidelity, Love
Lily of the Valley (toxic)	Happiness
Magnolia	Fidelity
Morning Glory	Happiness
Myrtle	True Love
Queen Anne's Lace	Love, Unity
Primrose	Wishing, Good Luck
Red Root	Passion
Rhododendron (toxic)	Passion
Rosemary	Love, Protection, Fidelity
Rue	Fidelity
Tansy	Fidelity
Trillium	Good Luck, Blessings
Violet, White	Romance
Violet, Purple	Passion
Wheat	Fertility, Abundance

If the families of the couple do not get along together, there are two magickal remedies for keeping quarrels from spoiling the wedding. The first is to sprinkle plain white sugar on the floor or ground where the ceremony will take place. Walking over the sugar will magickally "sweeten" the sour feelings. The other remedy is to take two rifles or shotguns (long barrels work best for this spell), one belonging to the head of each clan about to be joined through marriage. Cross the rifles together near the entryway to the place where the wedding is to be held to magickally cross out quarrels. These spells are not permanent solutions to family feuds, but will keep tempers at bay until the festivities are over.

In accordance with the Old English ditty, "Something old, something new, something borrowed, and something blue," the Appalachian bride adheres to these old ways. Her something old is most often a small heirloom piece of furniture or jewelry from an older female relative; the "something new," her dress or her shoes; and the "something blue," her flowers or some other personal decoration. It is the "something borrowed" which has the greatest significance in an Appalachian wedding. In keeping with the local beliefs that items used by others absorb their owner's good or bad fortune (for example, see the omens and taboos having to do with shoes in Chapter Five), the mountain bride would not think of going to the altar without carrying some small token loaned to her by a woman whose marriage has been happy and fruitful. Though few today might recognize it as such, by carrying this memento, the bride brings good luck into her own marriage through none other than sympathetic magick.

The mountain wedding is as likely to take place in someone's home or outdoors as it is inside a church, and, in the past, marriages were widely attended all-day *and* all-night affairs. After the ceremony itself is feasting, drinking, and dancing, which culminates in the great fun of "bedding the bride" and the "charivari."

For the bawdy ritual of bedding the bride, all the married women escort the new bride to her chambers and help her prepare for bed. Of course this is done amid off-color jokes intended to bring a blush to the girl's cheek. Essential to the arrangement is putting shoes, slippers, or some other type of foot gear within easy reach of the bed since it is very bad luck for the new bride to allow her feet to touch the bare floor before sunrise. When the bride is in bed and ready for her groom, the women announce this to the married men, who then carry the new groom up to the bedroom and literally toss him in with his bride. The crowd, of course, must pretend that it will not disperse until they see proof of the consummation of the marriage.

The bedding the bride practice can be directly traced to the sacred marriage rituals which were part of Pagan fertility rites in which the union of the God and Goddess ensured that the fertility cycle of the seasons would continue unimpeded. Until only about 200 years ago, some houses of European royalty were subjected to the bedding the bride ritual, only the crowd would literally stand just out of sight of the bed to make sure their king, the representative of God on earth, was doing his duty to them through his new wife.

Though many origins have been hypothesized for the charivari, it seems to be a uniquely American ritual still practiced in many rural locales. While the consummation of the union is presumably taking place unseen, wedding guests assemble all manner of pots, pans, noise makers, and musical instruments, and then regroup back under the window of the couple's bedroom to make all the racket they can. The ruckus is kept at an ear-splitting pitch until the couple shows themselves at a door or window, at which point they are cheered, toasted, and serenaded. Often in the midst of all the revelry, when the opportunity presents itself, the younger men will kidnap the groom and spirit him away to the woods where they leave him blindfolded to find his own way back home to his bride.

Of course, if any traveling is to be done the next day by the couple, the ubiquitous shoes are tied to the back of the wagon or other vehicle. Shoes dangling from a newlywed's car is a common sight all over North America, a prosperity rite handed down to us from the Anglo-Saxons.

The Magickal Wedding Ring

The precise origins of the wedding ring are unknown, though rings have been worn since pre-history to designate rank within a society. They were given at coronations and installations, and their use was even regulated by law in some countries, most notably in ancient Rome. In keeping with this practice, wedding rings might have first been used to identify the status of those who were bonded in marriage to another. The circular form of the ring, which has no beginning and no end, is symbolically linked to the magickal circle, the sacred space wherein spells have been cast and religious rites performed for many millennia. This never-ending circle made by the ring may also have once been intended as a symbol in its own right, one of undying love and fidelity.

Any piece of jewelry which is worn often by one person, and which has special meaning to that person, absorbs the personal energies from the wearer and will be applicable to the following ring spells. Keep in mind that, in Appalachia, it is the humble wedding ring which specifically is considered to possess magickal properties.

The wedding ring has the power to heal minor sores and cuts over which it is placed, so long as it can fully encompass the affected area. As mentioned in Chapter Three, a stye, an eye inflammation, is often treated with a wedding ring. Minor cuts, scratches, and moles are also treatable with the ring.

Probably the most common magickal use for the wedding ring is in divination. You can roll the wedding ring to divine the answer to a simple yes or no question. Hold the ring on its edge and roll it out in front of you. If it breaks left, your answer is no; if it breaks right, the answer is yes. Wedding rings have also been tossed like a coin, where and how they land giving the diviner some clue to the question asked. If the ring spins on its edge, the answer is positive; if it spins flat, the answer is negative. And if it rolls into a tight counterclockwise circle, the answer is no, but a tight clockwise circle is a yes.

Mountain women are fond of making pendulums out of their rings by plucking a single strand of their hair and tying one end to the ring (try substituting a strand of thin natural-colored thread if your hair is not long enough for this).[6] The ring should be held suspended in front of you by the hair and allowed to twist itself out of any kinks which might affect its movement. When the ring is still, focus on a question you have and wait for the pendulum to make a definite movement. There are several schools of thought for the meanings of the ring's movements, and you may already have your own in mind. For those who do not, begin your experiments by using the following as a guideline:

Pendulum Movement	Interpretation
Circles Wide Clockwise	Absolute Affirmative
Circles Wide Counterclockwise	Absolute Negative
Circles Clockwise	Probably Positive, Yes
Circles Counterclockwise	Probably Negative, No
Moves Right and Left	Stop, Uncertain, Bad
Moves Up and Down	Continue, Good
Moves Corner to Corner	Unseen Influences at Work
Switches Directions	Danger, Too Much Unknown

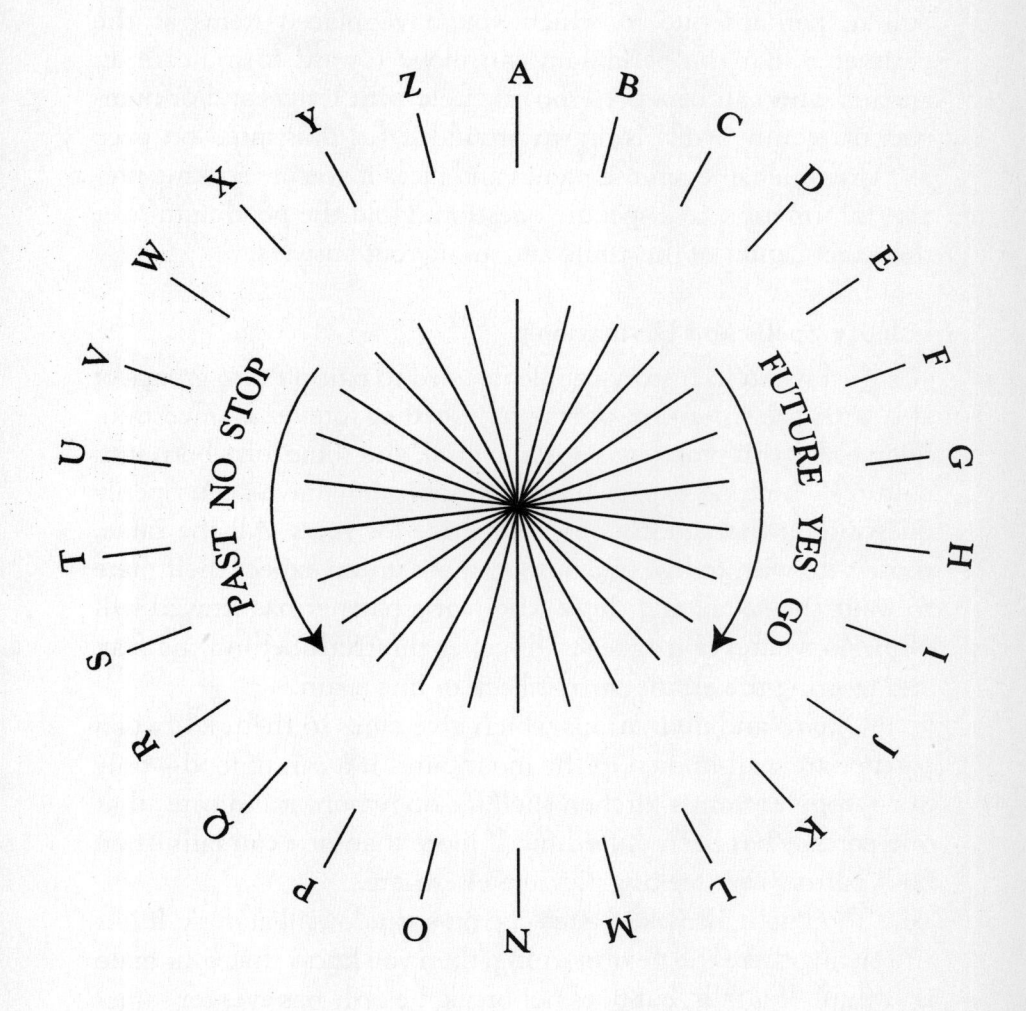

A Pendulum Circle

You can also set up a specific circle in which you use the pendulum, perhaps one in which you have placed items at the perimeter that the pendulum can move toward to indicate an answer. This can be a posterboard circle with letters and/or numbers or picture symbols drawn around it (as illustrated on page 141), or you can even use names and faces if you are seeking precise information to a specific question. Hold the pendulum over the exact center of the circle and await your answers.

Fidelity Spells and Divinations

Just when in history people decided to pair off into groups of two with the intention of staying together forever is uncertain. Even today this practice is not universal, and some folks born into cultures which do expect life-long monogamy have been openly questioning the validity of the practice for years. All the same, those who wish to live in a monogamous union expect their mate to want the same, and those who fear a partner has strayed will often do whatever it takes to discover the truth behind the fear, and to bring the errant partner back in line again.

Omens and divinations which give clues to the fidelity of a partner are well-known in the mountains. If a can of food—only one—topples from a kitchen shelf for no reason, it indicates that one partner has been unfaithful. If more than one can falls, then both partners are seeking pleasure elsewhere.

You might also place a tea cup on a windowsill at dusk. If it is still sitting there the next morning, then you know that your mate is faithful. If it falls, but does not break, he only has eyes for someone else, but if the tea cup cracks or breaks, then your partner is a total cheat.

Other popular tests to see if your mate is being faithful involve using your wedding ring as a divination device with the various methods discussed earlier in this chapter. Or you can place your wedding ring under the mattress you share with your partner, carefully marking where it rests. Sleep on it overnight with your mate beside you. The next morning check to see how many inches it has moved away from its original resting place. No more than two means your mate is faithful; two to five, he or she is merely thinking about someone else; six to nine indicates trouble is brewing. If the ring travels a foot or more, be assured your mate is seriously interested in someone else.

You can attempt to divine the name of your mate's new interest from a list of possible suspects by taking a poker or stick, and heating it in the fireplace or over a candle flame until it is red hot. Take the poker outdoors and write the name of the suspected spouse stealer on the ground where your mate will have to walk over it in order to get into your home. The name does not need to be visible, and, in fact, the spell will work all the better if it is not. If your mate complains later that night of having sore or burning feet, you have written the name of the right person. If there is no complaint, repeat the spell the following day with another name. Repeated efforts which yield no response either mean your mate is faithful, or that you just haven't come up with the right name yet.

By the time the mining industry came to the mountains, most of the rich lore and magick widely known to mine workers in Britain had been forgotten. However, one prevalent new belief which took its place says that if the head lamp on a miner's hardhat burns out while he is underground, it is a sure sign that his wife has taken another lover. Though the mines now employ many women, this omen does not seem to apply to them.

Spells for forcing your mate to remain faithful are also frequently practiced. Because these spells are a well-known part of Appalachian folk magick they are presented here, though the ethics of such practices—in other words, are they manipulative magick?—will have to be decided by each individual. My own thoughts on this are that yes, the spells are manipulation, and they should be avoided. If you want an exclusive relationship you would be best advised to find someone who shares that ideal from the start. Anyway, why would you want to hang on to someone if using manipulative magick is the only way you can keep them?

One really nasty spell for the wronged woman to try is to place fresh-picked rosemary under the mattress every night while visualizing it withering there in the heat and pressure. This will prevent the man from being able to function sexually with another woman as long as the herbs are replaced each day, and as long as the man remains unaware of their presence. (I once knew a *curandera*, or Mexican shaman, in Texas who swore by this same spell!) The old rosemary must be buried daily away from your home, or burned until there is nothing left but ashes.

Rosemary placed under a man's dinner plate will keep him happily coming home to you each night. This won't necessarily keep him physically faithful, but will limit his opportunities for roving.

A worried man may opt to place fresh mugwort under the mattress, a magickal cure for a woman's wandering eye. Ashes under the mattress will keep the wife coming home each night, and her emotions focused on her own home and man.

The rich blue wildflowers known as bachelor buttons can be gathered and burned with some of your mate's nail or hair clippings, symbolically severing his (or her) interest in the bachelor lifestyle. Bury the ashes where they will not be found by your partner, or the effectiveness of the spell may be lost. Or, you can take your own nail or hair clippings, mix them with those of your mate, wrap them in a dark green leaf, and bury them together near your home to ensure faithfulness. If you live in an older home, you might want to place this bundle under the floorboards of your bedroom for a more immediate effect.

While your mate is sleeping, wrap some fresh lengths of ivy around his or her wrist, entwining the other end around your bedpost, or use your own wrist if you have no posts. This practice may have roots in Pagan Europe where marriages and betrothals were sealed with a ritual known as handfasting, part of the rite involving the binding of the hands together. Make sure your mate remains unaware of what you are doing, and be careful to remove the ivy before sunrise. Do this for nine consecutive nights, starting on the waxing crescent moon, and your love will never stray.

The same kind of poppets which were described earlier in this chapter for use in love magick can be used to bring a wandering mate back home. As before, you will need to make two dolls, one to represent you and one to represent your mate. This time you should be sure to add some personal item to each poppet such as a handkerchief, hair ribbon, or other small token which will not be missed. Bind the dolls face to face with a red (for passion) or blue (for loyalty) string.

Take the poppets to the graveyard at midnight and bury them laying on their sides just inside the entrance. Mark the spot with a circle, which you draw with your own fingers. As long as the dolls remain undisturbed, your love will be loyal to you.

Endnotes to Chapter 6

1. Though I never tried it, I first heard about this divination from my grandmother, a woman who spent a great deal of time worrying about whether and when her granddaughters were going to wed.

2. This custom was faithfully portrayed in an episode of the "The Waltons" television series.

3. The primary mythic source is that of King Arthur's Guinevere, though there are others. In medieval Europe, nursery rhymes were often employed to hide magickal lore from the witch hunters. The spell, in a variant form, is given in the ditty: "The fair maid who on the first of May/ Goes to the fields at break of day/ And bathes in dew from the Hawthorn tree/ Will ever strong and handsome be."

4. For an example of adapting this spell to the beliefs of another magickal tradition, please see Chapter Eight.

5. For those interested in learning more about the magickal properties of plants, look into Scott Cunningham's *Encyclopedia of Magical Herbs* (Llewellyn, 1986).

6. For more on the use of pendulums, and on making a pendulum wheel, see my earlier book, *The Sabbats* (Llewellyn, 1994).

CHAPTER SEVEN

Fertility, Childbirth, and Children

I gave my love a cherry that has no stone,
I gave my love a chicken that has no bone,
I gave my love a ring that has no end,
I gave my love a baby with no cryin'.
—Traditional Mountain Song

Over the past 5,000 years, the miraculous bodily functions known as menstruation and pregnancy, which allow for the continuation of human life, have developed an increasingly ugly reputation. Menstruating women have been looked upon as unclean or dangerous, and often they have been punished merely for being born female by being separated for several days each month from their community, not being allowed to touch or be touched by others, or to come into direct contact with sacred objects. In pregnancy they were restricted to certain spheres of activity which would not "contaminate" food supplies or the home. These societies managed to forget that these taboos dated from a time when Goddesses were the supreme deities, and a woman who was bleeding or carrying a new life inside herself was considered to be Goddess-like, very powerful and respected.[1] While those of us living in the almost twenty-first century can scoff at the idea that any normal body function would render a person unsafe to be around, many of these beliefs still exist the world over.

Because men and women in Appalachia had to share the burdens of providing shelter and food, and because families lived in much closer quarters, a less rigid code of behavior was placed on menstruating and pregnant women than had been known in medieval Europe. The harsh, hardworking life of the mountain people just did not leave room for many taboos which would take a woman away from her daily chores. Still, some magickal beliefs and taboos concerning reproductive functions are found in Appalachia today.

Fertility Magick and Divination

In Appalachia, broken menstrual taboos were thought to have an impact on future fertility and so were carefully observed. A menstruating woman must never wash her hands, take off all her clothes, or bathe by immersing herself. However, this is an excellent time for her to learn magickal arts from a granny woman, or to gather healing herbs—a surviving belief from ancient times which teaches that a woman's magickal power peaks during this time. When all these menstrual do's and don't's are followed, a woman should be in good shape when she wants a child.

There are several omens to look out for which indicate when a birth will occur. Three robins coming to rest on the lawn of a newlywed couple means that a baby will arrive within one year's time, but three visiting wrens mean no birth will be forthcoming until at least the following year.

If a woman has trouble starting a fire in her hearth during the first month of her marriage, she will have trouble conceiving a child. If a newly married man drops his ax more than twice while chopping wood, his wife will have trouble getting pregnant.

A woman with thin thighs or knobby knees is considered to be a poor breeder, as is a man with large or dark nipples.

To foresee how soon it will be before you will become parents, you can take a corn husk doll, or a doll made of any other kind of natural material, to an old oak tree at sunset. In the event that no oak tree can be found, the tallest tree available will do nicely. One partner should place the doll as high in the branches as is easily accessible. Climbing to get there is okay, but not necessary. Both partners should spit at the base of the tree after uttering a charm such as:

Tall and ancient oak of the fertile earth,
How many months till three be at our hearth?

Both of you should walk away without looking back, and avoid making conversation about the doll. Get a good night's sleep, then return to the tree at sunrise to look for the doll. The number of feet the doll has fallen away from the trunk of the tree is how many months it will be until conception occurs. If the doll remains in the tree, it means no child will be conceived in the coming year.

You can find out how many children you will have in your lifetime by using a glass of water filled completely to the brim, a string, a stick, and your wedding ring, or any other evenly weighted ring which you wear frequently. Tie one end of the string to your ring, the other to the end of a stick, and suspend it over the glass of water. Ask aloud:

How many young ones will I bear
before this life of mine is over?

After you ask the question, lower the ring quickly into the water. Then wait and listen. The number of times the ring strikes the side of the glass is your answer.

If you are a woman who is having trouble conceiving, arrange to be the first female to set eyes upon a newborn and you will be the next mother. Or you might instead allow someone to lay a newborn on your own bed. Make love every night for a week afterward, and you will conceive.

To help boost your fertility, you can work a little sympathetic magick on your own behalf with an inexpensive packet of garden seeds. In a small mixing bowl, use your fingers to combine the seeds with a few drops of your blood—menstrual blood is most excellent—while visualizing the seeds as a representation of your fertile self. Allow them to sit overnight undisturbed. If you like lunar imagery, you can allow the light of the moon, the planet associated with fertility, to fall over them, though this is not the Appalachian way. The next day, plant the seeds outdoors near your home, or in an indoor planter. As they grow, so should a baby.

Magick relying on the assistance of ancestor spirits is very ancient, and from this practice comes one of the more unusual Appalachian fertility spells.[2] Take some flower seeds, preferably ones which will blossom red like blood, and go to the grave of a forebear. Men should try to go to a male ancestor, and women to a female one. If this is not possible, try to seek out the grave of someone older and wiser whom you once admired; perhaps that of a mentor or teacher. Once you have selected the grave, kneel upon it and, with your hands only, dig nine small holes. Plant a seed in each one, while praying to the ancestor to help in allowing your line to continue. In keeping with Appalachian tradition, you may wish to leave the cemetery without looking back.

Return a few weeks later to the grave to check the results of your effort. The number of plants which eventually spring from the holes indicates the extent of willingness on the part of the ancestor to intercede on your behalf. For example, if eight plants come up, your forebear is eager to work for you, but if you find only two sprouts then this ancestor clearly has little interest in whether your line continues or not. If you are unhappy with the results, you may repeat the spell at the graves of other ancestors, until you get the response you want.

After you have successfully enlisted the help of a concerned spirit, you should begin a concerted effort to conceive in which she or he is involved. Each night before you make love, call on the benevolent influence of the ancestor to aid you. I would suggest keeping nearby until you are successful a picture or small personal object which belonged to that ancestor. This will help keep your energies linked.

Pregnancy Taboos and Safeguards

There are many things a pregnant mountain woman must not do if she wishes to protect her unborn child. She must not admire her swelling figure in a mirror, she must not walk beneath a horse (though I have yet to figure out why she would want to), she must not allow her photograph to be taken, she must not spin wool, nor should she remove her wedding ring, regardless of how much her fingers swell. The expectant mother must avoid eating fish or tubers of any kind, or she will run the risk of dying in the birthing bed. She also should not cross a stream of running water, and, in some communities, it is even recommended she not bathe! Above all else, she must never walk through a cemetery if she wants her child to survive infancy.

The father of the child also has some taboos he must follow. He must not refer to the child by the word "it," but must call the baby a "he" or a "she"; nor should he eat potatoes after dark, spit in the house, or allow a black snake to cross his path.

If either partner transgresses these taboos, there is a likelihood that the child will not be born alive, or will not survive babyhood, or will carry some horrible blight throughout life as witness to his parents' carelessness.

Criminals in mountain communities will avoid pregnant women in their last months for fear of being discovered, since it is widely accepted that a baby will kick vigorously and erratically when the mother stands near a criminal. The more heinous the crime, the worse the kicking episode will be.

Clothing should not be made for the unborn child until the seventh month of pregnancy has passed, and no caps or bonnets should ever be made until after the birth, as it is believed these will magickally enlarge the baby's head, making for a very difficult birth.

Appalachian women are careful to control their urges during pregnancy, giving in to them only sparingly. Even though cravings for certain foods are a natural part of pregnancy, probably brought on by hormone shifts within the body, it is believed that if a woman gives in excessively to these cravings, the child will bear a mark of her weakness. For example, eating copious amounts of strawberries might produce a mottled red birthmark similar to that of the skin of a strawberry, while consuming large quantities of corn might produce a jaundiced baby.

Severe fright is another way in which a child can be marked for life, either to his advantage or his detriment. A century ago it was rumored that the mother of the famous sharpshooter Annie Oakley had been frightened by gunfire while carrying Annie, and that this accident produced her stunning gift for accuracy. Annie's is an example of a fright providing an advantage; just as often, the scare works against the child. For instance, if a mother has been startled by an animal or alarmed by a bad dream, the child may have troubles with that animal or object all his life, or might be born with a birthmark bearing its shape.

Some doctors today estimate that as many as eighty percent of all conceptions end in miscarriage; most of these happening so early on as to be unknown even to the mother.[3] Given these grim statistics, it is little wonder that so much birthing folk magick concerns how to prevent a miscarriage.

In the days before vascular micro-surgery, a woman who miscarried, especially during the second trimester, risked—at best—irreparable damage being inflicted on the uterine wall, or—the worst—a deadly hemorrhage. In Appalachia there remains a strong belief in axes as magickal tools which can prevent hemorrhaging. These are sunk deep into the floorboard under a laboring woman's bed until after her child is safely delivered, and it is clear that she will survive.

Sleeping with a rasher of bacon under the mattress, or eating meals without benefit of a knife, is also supposed to help prevent miscarriage.

Another way to thwart miscarriage is to carry a piece of mottled jasper in your left pocket. Commonly known as bloodstone, this red and green rock has long enjoyed a reputation as a bleeding preventative in Britain, and as such was used by soldiers and warriors, as well as by expectant mothers.

An expectant mother might also ask her partner to draw a talisman of some sort on her stomach using charcoal. This should be done at the new moon and be allowed to remain on the body until the moon is full, at which point it can be washed off and redrawn at the start of the next lunar cycle. If you are interested in

Pentagram
5-pointed Star

St. Bridget's Cross

Hexagram
6-pointed Star

Eight-spoked Wheel

Solar Wheel

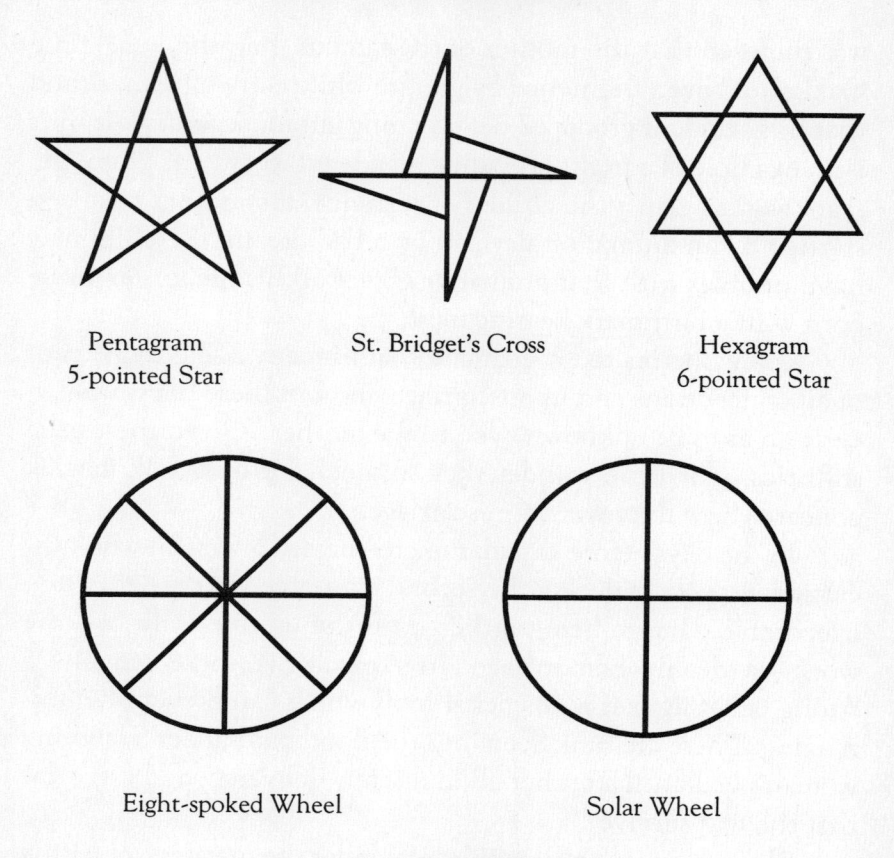

Ancient Symbols

trying this spell, body paints or non-toxic watercolor markers will work better than charcoal and are much less messy. The symbols chosen for the temporary talisman run the gamut from modern religious symbols such as the Christian or Latin cross, easily the most often-used glyph, to animal or plant representations. Occasionally these symbols include very old glyphs from Pagan Europe. Some mountain people still view these as magickal emblems of protection, though their original meanings having been long forgotten. These include the six-pointed star (ancient representation of the creator now used as a symbol for the Jewish faith), the pen-

Fertility, Childbirth, and Children

tagram (the five-pointed star which symbolizes Paganism), the eight-spoked wheel (marking the eight solar festivals of the Celtic Pagan year), the St. Bridget's Cross (resembling a swastika and once used as a symbol for the Irish Goddess Brighid), or a solar wheel (representing balance, stability, and the solstices and equinoxes). The symbol(s) you choose should have meaning to you and your partner, for only then will it be effective. Illustrations of these ancient symbols appear in this chapter (opposite), and should be intimately familiar to those who practice European-based magick/religions. The following list contains a few of the talismanic symbols which have used in the mountains, along with their most common meanings:

Symbol	Meaning
Bear Tracks	Gift of Inner Strength
Bees	Abundance and Safety
Circle	Protection
Fish	Gift of Divine Guidance
Solar Wheel	Protection
Spider	Blessings of Motherhood
Moon	Motherhood
Latin Cross	Divine Protection
Laurel Leaves	Protection of Fetus
Oak Leaves	Gift of Inner Strength
Pig's Tail	Protection, Gift of Safe Birth
Raccoon Tracks	Good Fortune
Stars and Suns	Protection, Blessings
Star of David	Protection, Blessings
Swine Tracks	Abundance
Webs	Protection from Miscarriage
Wolf Tracks	Gift of Strong Family Ties
X (the letter)	Driving Out Negativity

Another Appalachian belief is that keeping plenty of food stores in the house will help prevent miscarriages. This may have its roots in some ancient concept about the soul of a child lurking around awaiting its birth, and first wanting to make sure it has a secure home. If the child's soul witnesses evidence of poverty, then it might look elsewhere for parents, and the unborn fetus be miscarried.

Washing the stomach in animal blood, or anointing it with swine feces, are also well-known miscarriage preventatives, but, for health reasons, these are not recommended.

As the birthing time grows nearer and there is less to fear from miscarriage, a parent's concern naturally turns toward the actual birthing and curiosity about the sex of the child. Modern medicine, with ultrasound and amniocentesis, has taken the mystery out of wondering about a baby's gender, but in the very recent past, almost everyone—everywhere—knew of at least one omen or divination which would provide the answer.

To determine the gender of your unborn child, have your partner or a friend take a wedding ring, and tie it to a strand of your own hair (or to a thin piece of natural-colored thread if your hair is not very long) and suspend it over your bare belly. If it rotates counterclockwise, the child is a girl, clockwise, a boy.

You can also try counting back to determine the night on which you most likely conceived. Your obstetrician can help you pick this date to within a day or two, if you are unsure. If you conceived within three days either side of the full moon, you are carrying a girl, otherwise it is a boy.

Another divination to determine gender requires having the pregnant woman sit with her back toward a fireplace while two other people sit on either side of her, trying to kindle a flame in the hearth. If the side to the mother's left takes first, the child is a girl, but if the right side burns first, the baby is a boy. If you do not have a fireplace, you can have the expectant mother lie down while you set two identical candles burning on either side of her belly. If the right side burns out first she will have a girl, if the left burns out first, it will be a boy. If either flame dies out of its own accord before naturally burning down, it is a bad omen for the birth.

There are two mountain omens concerning the actual birth to be watched for. The first tells that if the baby's father appears to manifest the more unpleasant symptoms of pregnancy, such as morning sickness or backaches, the mother's labor is likely to go easily. If she bears these symptoms alone, she will have a difficult birth. The other says that if the mother has trouble getting up out of chairs, the labor will be an easy one, but if she remains spry, the labor will be hard on her.

The Folk Magick of Childbirth

The nine months of waiting are over, all the divinations have been done, and all the taboos avoided. The new baby is finally about to be born, and mountain magick continues to play a part in the event. As the process of labor begins, there are still omens to watch for and taboos to observe.

First of all, in a house of birth, there should be no item which contains a knot of any kind—not a forgotten apron string, a rope, or even a ball of knitting yarn. To leave knots is to risk the knotting of the umbilical cord (via negative sympathetic magick), cutting off the baby's oxygen supply, which can cause brain damage, or even death.

A concerned loved one will sometimes drive a nail into one of the bedposts. This use of metal to deflect evil influences was brought to the mountains directly from Celtic Ireland, where similar methods have been employed for centuries to protect against baneful faeries.

Birth can be speeded along by greasing the mother's thighs with lard, having her drink hot pepper tea, or by inducing sneezing fits with pepper and other aromatic herbs. Chicken feathers might also be burned nearby, since the smoke is believed to induce relaxation and ease birth pains.

The easy-to-come-by herb, rue, may also be employed to help bring on contractions when labor is either late in coming, or the process slows down. It is most often given in the form of a strong tea, which is sipped over the course of about an hour. The plant has been proven to contain a chemical which causes the contraction of smooth involuntary muscles such as those in the uterus.

Other magickal assistance may come from the granny woman, who also acts as midwife. She might place a white stone under the center of the mattress, which will help stop the birth pains, or she might place a very sharp knife under the bed to magickally chop the pain into manageable pieces. The granny woman might also be skilled with "the healing touch," what we know today as acupressure. She will skillfully press on key points of the body to ease the pain and speed the birth. Those key areas to be manipulated are the earlobes, upper arms, the ankles, and the feet.

After the birth, if this is the mother's first child, the granny woman will carefully count the number of lumps or knots along the umbilical cord to determine the total number of pregnancies the mother will have in her lifetime. She takes special note of lumps which are exceptionally small since these may indicate future miscarriages or stillbirths.

The granny woman then tends to the newborn, virtually ignoring the mother who, to avoid uremic poisoning, according to tradition, must lie in her unclean bed for at least three hours before having the sheets changed.

In keeping with an ancient and widespread belief, any child born with a caul (a thin membrane over his or her face) is gifted with special powers. A local witch or granny woman is likely to be the authority who decides how to dispose of the caul. In some mountain communities, the caul is dried and preserved, so that the child can burn it upon reaching his thirteenth birthday. In other places, it is buried or burned immediately. The grannies will also determine, usually through trance work (altered states of consciousness) or through a divination of some type, if there are any taboos the parents must observe in raising this special child. After all, the witches and granny women have a vested interest in the newborn since, in all likelihood, the child will grow up to be a magickal leader in the community.

After the newborn has been cleaned, and is breathing on his own, he might be taken by his heels and shaken to keep him from developing the condition unique in mountain lore called becoming "liver grown." This is a mistaken belief that the liver can attach itself to the wall of the abdomen, causing all sorts of pain and complications throughout life. Medical science has proven there is no such condition as being liver grown, so you need not worry about, or attempt this dangerous practice, which has been known to break the neck or spine of the newborn. A somewhat less dangerous, but still painful, test for the "disease" is to simultaneously pull the child's right hand behind his back to touch his left foot, and the left hand to the right foot. It is believed that if this feat can be accomplished at will anytime during the baby's first year, the child will be free from liver problems. Again, there is no such thing as being liver grown, and any attempts to check for or prevent it may result in the serious injury or death of an infant. The practice is mentioned here because, until very recently, it was quite prevalent in the mountains, and needs to be mentioned as common folk practice which has—thankfully—died out.

Magick and Omens for and about Babies and Children

Children born in Appalachia around the turn of the twentieth century faced a forty-percent mortality rate.[4] Anxious parents were always on the lookout for omens about their child's longevity and worked on spells to protect their lives.

In Appalachia, clocks or watches are never given as birth gifts because of a belief that they become bound to the life of the newborn and whatever befalls the clock will befall the child. Call to mind the folk song about the grandfather clock which goes, "and it stopped short, never to run again, when the old man died." Anyone thoughtless enough to present such a gift will likely see it destroyed before their eyes.

A baby born with teeth is a bad omen for the entire household. In many mountain communities, the child itself is suspect, thought to be possessed by a demon. Common remedies to restore the rightful soul to the child's body have their roots in the faery beliefs of the Celts who accepted that faeries called changelings could replace a newborn baby. Most of these remedies are dangerous and involve torturous practices which border on child abuse and should NEVER be attempted. Among these barbaric rituals are blowing smoke into the baby's mouth, sticking it with a hot pin, and leaving it outside overnight.[5] Safer methods of protection include giving the child a drink of rainwater collected overnight in a church yard; bathing it with a cloth into which some rue or basil has been sewn (there is some evidence that both of these herbs were also used in Celtic purification rituals); or anointing its head, stomach, and feet with an oil into which a drop or two of homemade whiskey has been added.

It is good luck to get as many hand-me-downs as possible from children who are healthy and happy, but the clothing must then be passed on to another baby and never returned to the original owner's family, or the luck they brought will vanish.

If a baby is crying for no reason, and a south wind is blowing, it is an ill omen for the child, but if it is a north wind there is nothing to worry about, since mountain babies often cry for no reason in a north wind. The best remedy is to distract the infant until the wind changes directions.

Wherever poverty and malnutrition are evident, so is the mysterious infant "disease" known as the Failure-to-Thrive Syndrome. Babies with this syndrome cannot be diagnosed with any known illness, yet they grow weaker with each passing month, often refusing food and showing little interest in their surroundings. Most of them die before reaching their first birthday. My own father exhibited these frightening symptoms in the first few months after he was born in an Appalachian coal mining town. My grandmother, a college-educated woman who looked proudly down upon the mountain susperstitions, was growing frantic. When a neighbor suggested she feed her baby a diet of sugar and cream boiled in well water, she was just desperate enough to give it a try. She had been told that not only would her son thrive on this mixture, but that it was an old custom to feed this concoction at least once during a baby's first year to ensure the child a sweet and abundant life. When my grandparents moved to Indiana a few months later, my father was a healthy, robust toddler. By looking at his first birthday photograph, with his plump fists and chipmunk cheeks, no one would ever guess that anyone once feared he would not live to see that day.

In the health-conscious '90s, the thought of feeding a child refined sugar and fat-laden cream makes us cringe. Even so, we can use the magickal imagery of that mixture to create a mountain-flavored blessing. Sugar symbolizes a wish for a sweet life; the cream, the desire for abundance (which, in the mountains, usually means a wish that the child will never know hunger). The use of well water may harken back to old Europe where wells were symbolic of the mother Goddess, who would naturally have a soft spot in her heart for children. Mix the three items together in a small bowl while pouring all your dreams and wishes for your baby into them. Dip your fingertips in it, then place a small bit of the mixture on the baby's forehead as you state aloud this, or a similar blessing:

> *Child of my heart and soul, I wish you a sweet life full of happiness, one in which you never know hunger or want. I offer you this blessing with the eternal love only a* (insert father, mother, or relationship of other individual who is making the offering) *can give.*

You may also anoint other parts of the child's body as your spiritual tradition or personal tastes dictate. For instance, anoint the forehead, shoulders, and stomach to mimic the sign of the Christian cross; or the forehead, shoulders, and knees to make a pentagram. Any leftover mixture can be bottled and the bottle placed in the baby's room (out of reach, of course) as a talisman of good will.

Newborns and young children can also be magickally protected against a host of evil influences and illnesses. A child is never handed through a window for fear of marking him for life as a thief. If this happens, the child must be passed back through the window the other way before he is taken through the door again.

Fingernails are not cut until the first birthday, and the hair not until three years of age. Since mountain lore tells us that there is no really safe way to dispose of these clippings, and since they can be used to level curses against their owner, it is always best to wait until the child is older and better able to defend itself before those first trimmings. Just to be extra safe, the clippings should be burned to ashes, not buried where they might be discovered.

Either the herb yarrow or pixie lichen moss can be hung on a crib where it will drive away curses or ill-wishes from the jealous. A nail driven into the crib will also work.

Baby blankets can be embroidered or quilted with magickal protective symbols (see Chapters Six and Seven for examples) which will protect the child while sleeping. Turning the child's clothes inside out at night will protect him from witches.

Having the child drink warm milk laced with a bit of chamomile each night before going to sleep will protect him from evil and preserve his life until dawn. Adding a touch of catnip will prevent bouts of nighttime colic. The herb asafetida will prevent disease when hung around the neck, and might work well for older children, but you should NEVER put anything around an infant's neck for any reason. If you want to use asafetida to protect the health of a young child or baby, try hanging the necklaces in the child's bedroom well out of his reach.

Divining a Child's Future

After your child has been adequately safeguarded, you can begin to look for clues to his or her future. If a mother dies giving birth, the child—especially if it's a girl—will be a gifted healer and will often be taken in tutelage by a granny woman or other local witch.

Children will have "a way" with animals if they are born between the winter solstice and Christmas Day. In some parts of the mountains these children are believed to be able to communicate with animals in their very early years, even to the point of understanding animal speech. This belief has its origins in folktales of Pagan central Europe which tell about animals who are permitted the powers of speech on the night of the solstice, and from Christian legends which tell us that on the night of the birth of Jesus, the animals of the earth were allowed to use human speech.

A child born in Capricorn will have to work hard all his or her life long, but one born in Leo will have an easier time. Children born on Friday are especially mischievous, and those born on Sunday exceptionally well-mannered. A child is thought to be most fortunate if he or she is born on a waxing crescent moon—about four days into the lunar cycle—regardless in which astrological sun sign they are born.

The weather at the time of birth is also very important in determining the newborn's future. A baby born on the morning of a light frost will have a gentle nature and calm demeanor. Snow falling at the time of birth indicates a reserved but generous personality. Babies born in a thunderstorm indicate that the child's future will also be stormy, and his disposition cranky. Babies born during a gentle rain are believed to be showered with blessings from heaven, and the rain is often collected for formal church baptisms, or for private blessings gleaned from a now-forgotten Pagan past.

You can create your own rainwater blessing for your child by anointing key parts of the body while asking your own deity(ies) to gift your child with things such as wisdom (asked for while anointing the head), love and compassion (asked for while anointing the chest), help in traveling a good life path (asked for while anointing the feet), a good singing voice (asked for while anointing the throat), or creative abilities (asked for while anointing the hands).

A popular divination for finding out how good your child will be with money, and how well he will prosper in life, can be performed with a silver coin (the purer the silver the better) on the child's first birthday. As soon as the child is up and about that morning, sit down in front of him and hand him the coin. If the child grasps at it too quickly, it may indicate greed; complete lack of interest may point to a lack of understanding of the value of money. If the child manages to take and hold onto the coin, he will be good at handling money and will prosper in life. However, if the coin falls from his grasp, it means that money will be forever slipping through his fingers and prosperity will not likely be part of his future.

Mountain families can determine what occupation or interests their child will have as an adult as soon as he learns to crawl. Simply select twelve items which represent a hobby, profession, or pastime, and arrange them on the floor in a large circle like the numbers on a clock face. The diameter of the circle should be about eight feet, but twelve is better if you have the room. The items you choose should be safe for the youngster to be around and handle, and should clearly indicate—in your mind—a specific vocation or interest. For instance, you might choose a book to represent life as a teacher, a baseball bat for an interest in sports, a notebook for a journalist, herbs for a gift in healing, a pen for a writer, a hammer for a carpenter, seed packets for a farmer, a scale for a lawyer, etc.

When you have assembled all the items, and arranged them around the perimeter of the circle, place the child in the center and leave the ring. Go far enough away that you will not influence the child to crawl in any particular direction, but remain close enough to observe his or her reactions. Whatever item the child crawls to, or in which he takes an interest, is indicative of future choice of occupation or hobby. If the child shows an equal interest in many items, it means he or she will be well-rounded and have a variety of interests and talents. If the child shows little or no interest in the items, it doesn't necessarily mean that you are raising a vagrant, just that you have not selected anything among your twelve items which represents the little one's course in life. Feel free to select a new set of twelve items and try the divination again the next day. (See the example of the baby divination wheel on page 166.)

Music has always been important to the people of Appalachia, and many of their stories and legends are preserved in their rich body of ballads and folksongs. Large community sings and dances were looked forward to and enjoyed until well into this century. To determine if your toddler will possess a musical talent, hand him or her a variety of musical instruments, one at a time, and observe how they are handled. A child who seems to have an intuitive knowledge of how to create sounds with them

Medicinal Plants for Doctor

Book for Teacher

Herbs for Farmer

Digging Tool for Miner

Clock for Hourly Labor such as Factory

Pen for Journalist

BABY

Religious Symbol for Clergy

Crayons for Artist

Baseball Hat for Athlete

Instrument for Musician

Hammer for Carpenter

Pot or Pan for Cook

Example of "What Will Baby Be" Divination

will have musical talent, those who do not seem to know what to do with them will not. The more instruments which can be correctly handled or sounded, the stronger the gift.

Testing for a good singing voice is determined by singing to the child and then gauging his reaction. A youngster who displays an interest, who claps or tries to keep rhythm, or who attempts to mimic the noises he hears, will be a good vocalist. Naturally, the better he does any or all of these things, the stronger the native talent. Even if your child shows little interest in your singing, don't give up! The mountaineers believe that singing frequently to a child will help musical talent to develop, even where it is not inborn.

The future physical appearance of a child is also determined by a host of divination methods which can be accurately gauged by the time the child is three years old. A child will have freckles if the hair is unruly, will be corpulent if he prefers to sleep on his stomach, skinny if he likes to eat berries, short if he has long toes, and tall if the feet are large for the body. Children who have colic at night will be pale-skinned, and those who like to sneak off into the woods will be hairy. Future disfigurement may be indicated by a child who is attracted to cutting tools at a young age (a logical assumption!), or who likes to hit and tease his siblings.

By taking your three-year-old to a nearby graveyard at midnight, you can catch a spectral vision of you child as he will appear as an adult. Go with the child to the oldest grave in the grounds, and the two of you walk in a circle around it seven times clockwise. You may want to chant a more elaborate charm as you circle, just to help open your psychic centers. Try something like:

>*Past and future in unbroken ring,*
>*Into my sight will come this e'en,*
>*This small (boy or girl) will grow to be,*
>*Whatever is now shown to me.*

After you make the last round of the grave, hold the child against your chest so that his head rests just below your field of vision. Face west and close your eyes for a few seconds, then open them, peering into the near distance over the child's head. A vision of the child as he or she will be in the future should be seen there. After the vision has appeared, lay to rest any spirits who may have been stirred up by your action—and who could wish to interfere with a particularly reassuring vision—by walking seven times counterclockwise back around the grave.

Endnotes to Chapter 7

1. French, Marilyn. *Beyond Power* (New York: Ballantine Books, 1985), pp. 91-99.
2. This spell is unusual from the standpoint that the sturdy fear of ghosts and spirits prevalent in the region makes these types of spells virtually unknown.
3. Lachelin, Gillian C. L. *Miscarriage: The Facts* (New York: Oxford University Press, 1985), introductory material.
4. Caudill, Harry M. *Night Comes to the Cumberlands: A Biography of a Depressed Area* (Boston: Little, Brown and Co., 1962).
5. McCoy, Edain. *A Witch's Guide to Faery Folk* (St. Paul, MN: Llewellyn Worldwide, 1994).

CHAPTER EIGHT

Integrating Appalachian Folk Magick with Your Own Magickal Lifestyle

*Sometimes I feel like a motherless child,
A long way from home.*
—Traditional Southern Lament

Folk magick has always tended to be a solitary practice, one intimately associated with the people of the land. You do not have to be part of a magickal study group, coven, or other occult organization to use any or all aspects of Appalachian folk magick in your daily life. Certainly this does not mean that groups should hesitate to use or adapt solitary folk spells into their routine practice. Many do with great success; it's just not a requirement.

It is a given that at least a few people who were practicing some form of magickal lifestyle in Europe, perhaps even religious

Witchcraft, immigrated to the Appalachian Mountains. Immigration is how the vestiges of the Old Religion spread to this country in the first place. If you practice Witchcraft or Paganism, and are wondering about ways of adapting mountain-style rituals into your own practice, you'll find this as easy as changing a few words here and there and adding gestures. For example, if you want to add some mountain flavor to your memorial ritual for the dead you might consider using the mountain colloquialisms "lych," "gorm," or "haint" where you might otherwise say "earthly shell," "soul," or "spirit."

Praying Rocks

One feature of the Appalachian magickal landscape which has nearly vanished, but one which is easily adaptable anywhere, is the use of a praying rock. Even today, in the most rural areas of the mountains, local witches and/or religious leaders routinely go to pray at large stones, partially embedded in the earth, which are found in natural settings near their homes. The mountaineers are usually aware of these sites, and respectfully stay clear of them unless needing to request prayer. Around the praying rocks are a collection of smaller stones, each one representing a person and need which is being worked on by the witch or preacher. The symbolism at work here is not unique. Items left at sacred places in the hope that they help the need reach the ears of a benevolent deity are to be found the world over. The principle is even at work in churches, where votive candles are lit and left burning by penitents. An interesting story about communal concern for a praying rock which was destroyed to make room for new construction can be found in *Foxfire 9* (Doubleday and Co., 1986).

You can create one of these sacred sites on your own land, or in your home, by setting aside a place which you designate as a sacred spot for calling upon divine intervention. This can be built around a potted plant, in the crook of a tree branch, the corner of a garden, on an empty bookshelf which has been adorned with religious items, or even a large rock in your yard. To ask for divine help, take another item, such as a small stone, a seed, candle, or coin, and carry it to that spot. Then ask your own God/dess for assistance in whatever manner you feel is appropriate. Keep the item you have brought with you in your hands, or in contact with your body in some other way, while you are making your petition, so that the stone can fully absorb your energies and need. When you have finished, leave the item behind to continue working for you after you are gone.

Appalachian Theme Gatherings

If you are one of those magickians who works alone on a regular basis, and who has access to few, if any, people with whom to share your newfound interest in Appalachian-style folk magick, you may want to try a trick of which I am very fond for bringing others into your world. Throw a party!

Send out invitations announcing that you are having an Appalachian theme party. Encourage costumes if you like, but don't be surprised if your friends show up in everything from period prairie-type garb to something they feel is stereotypically "hillbilly." Ask that they all bring along a favorite ghost story or tall tale to tell, explaining later that this was an integral part of mountain gatherings. Everyone loves a fortune teller at a party, so feel free to use some of the Appalachian divinations on your guests. It doesn't matter if those you read for believe in precognition, or if they think it's all in fun. You will know differently, and you will get a chance to test your divination skills. (Believe me, if you get things right someone *will* tell you.)

Don't hesitate to experiment with some down-home cooking for your party. Appalachian fare is simple, but marvelously seasoned with native herbs, and should appeal to most palates. See Appendix B for some traditional recipes and other cooking ideas.

If you want to keep your deeper interest in folk magick a secret, don't worry that this type of party will expose you. Informal gatherings naturally and immediately put people at ease. Unless you want someone to know there is more to your sudden interest in Appalachian ways than meets the eye, they would probably never guess. The whole point of the gathering is for you to introduce your interest in folk magick to the people you care about in a way which is non-threatening for them. The party also allows you to indulge in your magick and feel connected with it on the deeper level that communal celebrations naturally provide. The trick to making it work is for you not to take it all too seriously. Remember your guests are just there to have a good time. If they learn something, great; if not, no loss. Most will probably not know just how deep your involvement with magick is, nor do they need to know. The purpose will be served for both of you and no one will be hurt.

Introducing Children to Appalachian Magick

Children may best be introduced to Appalachian folk magick through hearing the tall tales of the mountain people, and through practical use of the folk games and toys mountain children have played with for decades. Two books which will help you impart these things to your children are *Tall Tales From Old Smokey* (Southern Publishers) and *The Foxfire Book of Appalachian Toys and Games* (Doubleday). With a little imagination, many of the toys can be turned into divination devices that children can use and enjoy. For instance, a simple wooden top can become a divination device by painting it with symbols meaningful to the child. Show the child how to ask a question or voice a concern, then spin the top while concentrating on what was asked. After the top comes to rest, the position in which it lands (i.e., what symbol the top is leaning on, or which one is facing upright), can indicate the answer to the question, or offer insight into an issue.

Choosing Appalachian Folk Spells for Your Own Use

Actual folk magick is even easier to integrate into your life than are ritual or group events. As you read through this book, you may wish to have a list handy of the types of needs you currently have, so that you can make notes of the related spells, divinations, or other practices which interest you. Jot down your current needs, along with the page numbers of ideas which appeal to you as you come to them. If you are already a practicing Witch or magickian, you probably have some type of magickal diary or Book of Shadows for this purpose. Making notes will help you locate ideas that interest you later on when you are searching for the perfect spell. When you decide it is time to enlist magickal help for your need, you can refer back to the list to see if any of the spells still appeal to you, or if you wish to look elsewhere. Sometimes a particular spell will strike your fancy at a particular time, and I have found that this is often the best one to use if the need is immediate. At another time, it may not feel quite so right, but you will want to keep it filed safely away for possible later use.

If you follow a spiritual tradition which seems to have nothing in common with the Appalachian heritage (i.e., Anglo-Celtic as filtered through a bit of "down-home" religion) and are concerned about adding it to your own practices, don't be. The magick of the common folk has never been a static entity, nor is it the sole property of any one people. Over the centuries, it has crossed many cultural boundaries, been reshaped, reinterpreted, added to, subtracted from, lost, and then rediscovered. The important thing is that, for many people, it works. Adding some or all of the folk magick of Appalachia to your current magickal repertoire will only enhance your appreciation for your craft. It will never detract as long as you alter the practice to conform to the ethics and practices of your own faith.

Examples, Precautions, and Guidelines for Adapting Specific Spells

As you may have noted, many of the spells found herein involve using the grounds of, or items taken from, a graveyard as a focus for the magick. Unless otherwise stated, the spells presented here are written down just the way they have been performed in Appalachia, or as nearly as can be gleaned from extant sources. Most of them come without any offerings made to, or permissions asked of, the cemetery's spirits. To present the spells any other way would not be true to the magickal feeling of the region, and to arbitrarily add these non-native practices would make the folk magick into something other than what it is (i.e., becoming Teutonic magick or Santerian magick with a thin veneer of Appalachian flavor tossed on as a colorful topping). To the minds of some magickal adepts, this oversight presents a situation considered tricky, or perhaps even dangerous, depending upon how one views this space. However, these hindrances can be overcome by adapting the graveyard spells to conform with the requirements of your specific spiritual tradition, or with the way you personally view the power behind the cemetery.

The Power from a Place Inbetween Places

The Celts believed that the most magickally potent places were those which fell "inbetween"; in other words, locations not clearly belonging to one world or another. These places included the edge of the seashore, tidal basins, cave openings, riverbanks, doorways, and burial grounds.

Many magickians who base their working philosophy on Celtic ideology will work in graveyards, viewing them as merely another place of "inbetween" power. They see graveyards as part of our physical landscape, but still not wholly of this world since they also belong to the realm of the dead. Rarely is reciprocity given or expected, such as leaving an offering at the grave in exchange for the magick power taken away, and human discarnates are not expected to play a major role in the magick.

To incorporate added Celtic flavor in your folk spells, and in keeping with the mountain ways as learned from Celtic ancestors, use the graveyard freely as a natural power spot. You might also consider liberally adding the symbolism of the Celtic sacred number three: repeat key phrases three times, call upon your deity(ies) three times, repeat ritual gestures three times, etc., when working your spells.

The Power of Hallowed Ground

A relatively modern view of the power of the graveyard comes from the belief that it is hallowed ground, land protected and set aside for a higher purpose. The idea that physical space can be marked off as holy is an ancient one, and is the origin of the magick circle in which most modern Witches and magicians work. To the minds of those who follow this thinking, the cemetery has been made holy by the words or rituals of the spiritual leaders who created and blessed the space. In Appalachia, this was probably done by a circuit-riding minister many years past. These magickians view taking power from the cemetery as being no different nor dangerous than taking holy water from a church. It is there to be used by those who come in reverence, seeking solutions to problems.

If you practice your faith in one of the Judeo-Christian religious traditions, this may be the easiest way to reconcile any uneasy feelings you have about cemetery magick. You may want to approach the cemetery with a prayer to your God, asking blessings and guidance in your efforts. If you like the idea of making offerings when divine assistance is either asked for or given, consider making a donation to your church or synagogue, perhaps specifying that it be used for cemetery upkeep.

Power from the Dead

For many modern magickians, the power of the graveyard is believed to come directly from the spirits of the dead, particularly when a spell involves ancestor spirits who presumably have a vested interest in the well-being of their descendants. Those who view the power behind graveyard magick in this way will often have ancestor shrines or altars at home on which they make offerings to enlist their ancestors' aid, or to ask for guidance from them in the form of a dream or a sign. They may even carry this need to pay them honor into the cemetery, and make offerings at the headstone or mausoleum of their ancestors, or at the marker of any other spirits whom they feel might wish to be of assistance.

In Chapter Five, there is a spell for stopping family quarrels which asks you to take nail clippings, or other items belonging to the combatants, to the cemetery to be placed on the grave of your oldest ancestor buried there. Note that the spell also asks you to leave bread behind as an offering. If you view the graveyard magick as coming from these discarnates, you may want to carry with you into the cemetery some other traditional ancestor offerings such as hair, wine, or perfumes. These can be used both as simple offerings and love gifts, or as a means of enlisting spectral aid. You might also want to perform some act of divination over the grave of a trusted ancestor or mentor to decide if this spell is harmful to others, or if it is something you should pursue further.

Power from the Graveyard Guardian

Another spirit who may need to be appeased is the guardian spirit of the cemetery. Many cultures have believed in the existence of this guardian, either in the form of a human discarnate, or as a graveyard deity such as Oya in the Yoruban tradition. As mentioned in Chapter Two, Appalachian folk beliefs teach that the burial ground is protected by the spirit of the last person buried there.

In that same chapter is a spell for divining how many deaths the community will have to endure in a season, a spell which uses the guardian as a catalyst for the answer. If you strongly believe in this being as the source of the power behind graveyard magick, you may want to bring offerings for him or her also. Take all your needed items to the cemetery, along with an offering for the guardian. Just before you reach the entrance to the graveyard, slow respectfully, calling out to the guardian with your mind. Laydown your other implements and, stepping over them, carry the offering to the entrance. These thresholds are magickal places in many European magickal traditions, and are the most likely place to encounter the guardian.

Without attempting to enter the grounds, tell the guardian why you are there and what it is that you want, reaffirming that you mean neither him, the grounds, nor other spirits any harm. Set the offering down in the entryway and stand still. Close your eyes, open your mind, and await an answer from the guardian as to whether you may or may not enter his graveyard. If you feel you have been denied permission to enter, don't force your way through. The guardian may not be acting arbitrarily, but perhaps protecting you from some other harm, such as an escaped criminal who has decided to hide there until dawn. Respect his decision and either wait until another night to ask again, or move on to another cemetery. In either case, it is considered bad form to take back your original offering. Leave it be, and try again later.

The guardian can also be your source of answers for divinations performed in the cemetery, or can be called upon to assist you in other magick performed there, the same way you might enlist the aid of an ancestor spirit.

For those who believe in the power of the guardian, he can be a potent friend or foe in graveyard magick, and should always be treated with respect.

The Power of Mother Earth

The last group of magickians with specific opinions on the power behind the graveyard are those who believe it comes from the fact that the graveyard is no more than what it appears to be—a part of Mother Earth. The people who follow this thinking are most often called "green witches," people who revere the land and work their magick within their personal ecological ideology. Eclectic Wiccans (a term for one branch of modern Witchcraft) also share some of these feelings.

When these magickians wish to take anything from the land, be it a stone, leaf, or herb, they feel they must ask permission of the plant or of the plot of ground from which they wish to take it. They also believe that they must make an offering in return. For example, in Chapter Six there is a spell with roots in East Anglia which asks that you take violets from a graveyard and bring them home to induce your love to come to you. Before those violets can be picked, the Mother Earth-oriented magickian comes to the cemetery prepared with a token of offering—usually this takes the form of a piece of bread, animal or bird feed, a special stone, or a coin. He will also bring a piece of clean white cloth, and a special cutting tool, usually a white-handled knife called a bolleen, which is used only for cutting magickal plants. The magickian will then make physical contact with the earth either by placing his hands on the ground, standing barefoot, sitting, etc. Closing his eyes, he will mentally reach out to the violets and attempt to let them know what he wishes of them, and why he needs their sacrifice. After a few minutes he will receive a telepathic answer, either yes or no. If the answer is no, the magickian will either rethink the spell, or move on to another patch of violets.

If the answer is yes, he mentally thanks the plants for their sacrifice, and begins cutting only what he needs, making sure not to destroy the entire plant by taking too much from any one area. The cuttings are then placed on the white cloth so that they are not allowed to touch the ground again. Followers of this thinking believe that once the harvested plant is allowed to touch the ground, the power in the plant will be grounded back into the earth, making it useless for magick.

After all the cuttings are taken, the magickian thanks the violets again, perhaps even offering a special prayer of thanks to Mother Earth, and then he leaves the offering as a token of thanks.

One Last Word On Graveyard Magick

Be advised that many magickians, from many magickal traditions, avoid graveyard magick—period!—though this does not make their point of view on the matter either right or wrong. Certainly both sides in this issue have a notable history on which to draw. Only you can decide if this is a practice with which you want to experiment or not. If you do decide to go ahead with it, then you must decide what, if any, changes you need to make to the spells to conform them to your personal views, or your magickal tradition's viewpoints. No one else's feelings can guide you in this. You are the one who is taking the risks, and you are the one who will either reap the rewards or endure the retribution.

Though some of the Appalachian spells may strike us as quaint or silly, it must be remembered that they still possess magickal intent. Magick, regardless of its origin, is not a game or an amusement, but a method of shaping the reality in which we live, and it should never be entered into unadvisedly or without forethought.

The choices are yours to make. Choose wisely.

APPENDIX A

Resources for Making Mountain Magick

Creating a rustic, mountain atmosphere for Appalachian folk magick has become quite easy in recent years with the strong revival of country/folk music and crafts. All of these things, as well as dried herbs and essential oils, are readily available by mail order. Below are a few of the many sources available to the people interested in all aspects of Appalachian folk magick. When writing to any of the businesses listed here, please do them the courtesy of enclosing a self-addressed stamped envelope (SASE).

Dried Herbs and Roots

Capriland's Herb Farm
Silver Street
Coventry, CT 06238

Write for free price list of dried herbs and herbal books. Capriland also holds special classes on herb use and has herbal lunches at various times throughout the year. Reservations are a must!

Companion Plants
7247 N. Coolville Ridge Road
Athens, OH 45701

Catalog $2.

Dreaming Spirit
P.O. Box 4263
Danbury, CT 06813-4263

Natural, homemade incenses and resins, oils, and tools for using them. The $2 for their catalog is refundable with your first order.

Halcyon Herb Company
Box 7153 L
Halcyon, CA 93421

Sells not only magickal herbs, but also other items of interest to magickal folk. Current catalog $5.

Herbal Endeavors
3618 S. Emmons Avenue
Rochester Hills, MI 48063

Catalog $2.50.

Indiana Botanical Gardens
P.O. Box 5
Hammond, IN 46325

Sellers of herbs, teas, charcoal blocks, herbal medicines, and some books on alternative health care. Request free catalog.

Marah
Box 948
Madison, NJ 07940

Catalog, $1.

Mountain Butterfly Herbs
106 Roosevelt Lane
Hamilton, MT 59840

Write with SASE for current information and prices.

Sandy Mush Herb Nursery
Route 2, Surrett Cove
Lancaster, NC 28748

Has over 800 in-stock herbs, dye plants, and other foliage. Catalog contains helpful herbal tips as well as recipes. Catalog $4, refundable with your first order.

Stones and Gems

Lapidary Journal
P.O. Box 80937
San Diego, CA 92138

This is a publication for rock collectors which contains information on stone origins and their lore. It also contains ads from companies which sell stones, tumblers, jewelry mountings, etc. Write for subscription information.

Musical Resources

Anyone Can Whistle®
P.O. Box 4407
Kingston, NY 12401
(800) 435-8863

This "Catalog of Musical Discovery" carries unique instruments from around the world, many of which include tapes and/or instruction books for learning to play. Often featured are autoharps and handcrafted dulcimers, both popular mountain folk instruments. Write for catalog.

Mountain Sound Productions
3148 Bolgos Circle
Ann Arbor, MI 48105
(313) 662-8187

Sells recorded mountain music and handcrafted folk instruments.

Folk Crafts

Candlechem
P.O. Box 705
Randolph, MA 02668

Sells candlemaking supplies, instruction books. Catalog, $2.00.

Country Folk Art Magazine
8393 E. Holly Road
Holly, MI 48442

Look for this bi-monthly publication on your local newsstand or write to the above address for subscription information. CFAM sponsors the Country Folk Art traveling craft show. Schedules are listed in the magazine.

Country Sampler
P.O. Box 352
Mount Morris, IL 61054-0352

This is another bi-monthly magazine which should be available on your local newsstand. If not, write to the above address for subscription information. CS sponsors the Country Peddler Show, a traveling folk art and craft show whose schedules are listed in the magazine.

Cumberland General Store
Route 3
Crossville, TN 38555
(615) 484-8481

Cumberland is an authentic old-time general store whose stock includes many things you probably thought they didn't make anymore. Among their offerings are cauldrons, cider presses, corn dryers, wine making supplies, candlemaking supplies, spinning wheels, craft books, folk instruments, oil lamps, canning supplies, folklore books, seasonal cookie cutters, cookbooks, hand-hewn bells, baskets, and fireplace supplies. Send $3.50 for the current catalog.

Dover Books
31 East 2nd Street
Mineola, NY 11501

Dover will send a free catalog upon request. Titles cover a broad range of subject matter including needlecraft, art, and nature crafts.

Quill-It
P.O. Box 1304
Elmhurst, IL 60126

Sells wheat and other craft grains, also instruction books. Send $1.00 for current catalog.

Travel Information

If you live near enough to the southern Appalachians to make a visit, you will gain a world of knowledge, as well as be able to pick up items for magick or ambience. If you are interested in traveling to Appalachia to experience it for yourself, there are many places to see and ways to see them which should fit almost any travel budget. The Great Smoky Mountains National Park and the Jefferson, Washington, Cherokee, and Pisgah National Forests all boast a variety of campgrounds from the most primitive to the "almost like home." The smaller parks, state parks, and national recreation areas, such as Cumberland State Park in Kentucky, not only have camping and hiking, but specialize in more elegant lodge accommodations. Houseboat rentals are popular on the mountain lakes and are perfect for large families or groups who prefer to share costs.

Since the addresses and toll-free numbers of the individual state/city tourist bureaus tend to change from year to year, the best place to get the updated information is from your local travel agent. Many will have free brochures on hand for you and they will likely have access to the numbers and addresses you would need for further information. Another listing of useful phone numbers (many toll free from within the continental United States) appears in the most recent annual edition of the *Rand McNally North American Road Atlas*.

If you are unsure about just where to go in Appalachia in order to really learn more about it, I would suggest beginning in Williamsburg, Kentucky, at the Appalachian Center. The center has museums, craft and artifact collections, a natural history area, and is on the edge of the Daniel Boone National Forest and other recreational areas.

Another good starting point is in Norris, Tennessee, at the Living Museum of the Appalachians. Here, traditional crafts can be seen in action, and the visitor gets a good dose of authentic mountain folk ways.

APPENDIX B

Traditional Recipes of Southern Appalachia

Traditional Appalachian cooking relies heavily on native seasonings to flavor home-grown vegetables, pork (the staple domestic animal), chicken, and game animals. At my first dinner in an Appalachian home, I was stunned to find myself sitting down to a meal of pinto beans and creamed corn, served with a side of homemade bread and butter. Not especially fond of either of the main courses, I tried to appear as gracious as is possible when one is mentally plotting how far it is to the nearest McDonald's. However, I was surprised to discover that, though the fare was simple and starchy, each dish was delicately seasoned with unusual combinations of mountain herbs.

Creamed Corn with Sage

1 pound corn, fresh or frozen	1 teaspoon salt
1 cup milk	¼ teaspoon pepper
2 tablespoons water	½ teaspoon sage
1½ teaspoons flour	Pinch dill

To one pound of corn, add all the other ingredients. Cook on stovetop in a large saucepan over medium heat, until corn is tender.

Honey Butter

½ pound sourwood or raw honey ¼ teaspoon sage
½ pound butter 1 teaspoon cinnamon

Combine the sourwood or raw honey with the butter. Add the sage and cinnamon. Whip until light and fluffy. Keep chilled when not in use.

Appalachian Baked Chicken

1 chicken, cut up Bit of Honey Butter
 (recipe above)

Pre-heat oven to 375° F. In a small baking pan, set out the chicken pieces so that they just touch each other. With a pastry brush rub a bit of Honey Butter (see recipe above) over the chicken. Begin baking while the following is prepared in a medium-sized bowl:

¼ cup ground walnuts 1 mild onion, finely chopped
½ teaspoon pepper ⅛ teaspoon wild ginger
1 finely diced potato ¼ cup Honey Butter
¼ teaspoon salt   (see recipe above)
½ teaspoon dried basil ¼ cup rosemary
½ teaspoon dried parsley 1 to 2 tablespoons cooking oil

Mix well and pour over the chicken. Allow to bake for 50–60 minutes or until golden brown.

Carrot Glaze

¼ cup brown sugar 2 tablespoons cooking oil
½ cup Honey Butter ¼ teaspoon dried goldenseal
 (see recipe above) ¼ teaspoon marjoram
⅛ teaspoon pepper Dash thyme

Combine the above ingredients in a medium-sized saucepan over low heat. Add sliced carrots, cover, and simmer until done.

Appendix B: Traditional Recipes of Southern Appalachia

Noodles with Okra

½ cup chopped okra
2 cups flour
¼ teaspoon baking powder
2 well-beaten eggs
3 tablespoons milk

Water
Chicken or beef stock
Chopped onions, to taste
Dash of salt

Remove stems from okra and chop leaves until very fine in texture (a blender can work wonders!). Combine the okra and the other ingredients, mixing the dough well, and then knead on a floured cutting board. Divide the dough into two or three smaller working pieces. With a rolling pin, roll out each section into thin pies. Generously flour the top of the dough and roll the pie up like a jelly roll. With a very sharp knife, begin cutting strips about ¼ to ½-inch wide. Unwind each strand and lay out on another floured board to dry overnight. The next day, boil the noodles for 45 minutes in water to which the following has been added: chicken or beef stock, chopped onions to taste, and a dash of salt.

Broiled Pork Chops

1–2 Pork chops per person
½ teaspoon dried nettles(*)
½ teaspoon dill
¼ cup cooking oil
⅛ teaspoon pepper

1 teaspoon sugar
½ teaspoon dried basil
¼ teaspoon wild ginger
½ cup rich milk

Marinate pork chops overnight in the above mixture. Set oven to broil and place chops on the broiling rack and baste. About halfway through, turn the chops over and baste again.

* Some people are sensitive to nettles and may choose to eliminate this ingredient.

Pinto Beans with Home Brew

1 pound of pinto or great northern beans	1 teaspoon apple cider vinegar
1 cup prepared catsup	¼ cup brown sugar
2 tablespoons wild mustard	½ cup water
1 tablespoon salt	Chopped onions to taste
½ cup whiskey or beer	Bacon or ham (optional)

Boil beans in water until soft. Drain the water. To the beans, add the other ingredients. Cover and cook over low heat for 45 minutes, stirring occasionally.

Basic Gingerbread Cake

Gingerbread in its many forms is probably the most popular of all desserts in the southern mountains. (You might try adding a cup or two of raisins, blueberries, or nuts to this cake for a unique flavor.)

1 cup lard or vegetable shortening	5 eggs, well beaten
	3¾ cups flour
1 tablespoon butter or margarine	2 level teaspoons baking soda
1 cup granulated sugar	3 teaspoons ground ginger
½ cup condensed milk or cream	¾ teaspoon ground allspice
½ cup buttermilk	⅓ teaspoon ground cinnamon
1 cup molasses	½ teaspoon ground cloves

In a large mixing bowl, beat the lard/shortening, butter/margarine, and sugar together until fluffy and light. Fold in the milk/cream, buttermilk, and molasses, blending well. Add the eggs to the mixture, being sure to blend well. In a separate bowl, combine all the dry ingredients. Slowly add the dry ingredients to the other mixture so that it can be mixed together smoothly. Cover and store the batter in the refrigerator for at least 24 hours.

When ready to bake, pour the batter into a 9 x 13-inch greased and floured pan, and bake in an oven pre-heated to 350° F. Bake for about 25 minutes, or until the cake starts to pull away from the sides of the pan.

APPENDIX C

Glossary of Terms

Acupressure—The art of applying pressure to one point on the body to cure a pain or illness in another.

Acupuncture—The ancient Chinese science of curing illness and/or pain by inserting needles just under the skin at strategic points which often seem to have nothing in common with the affliction. In Appalachia, pine needles are sometimes similarly employed.

Astral projection—The art of "leaving one's body" or "lucid dreaming" whereby someone in a trance state visits other locations, realms, or times. This is often referred to as traveling on the "astral plane," a place which is generally conceptualized as an invisible parallel world unseen in our own world of form.

Astrology—The study of and belief in the effects which the movements and placement of planets and other heavenly bodies have on the lives and behavior and activities of human beings, animals, and plant life.

Aura—The life-energy field surrounding all living things that can be seen and interpreted by those trained in the art.

Bealtaine—Also spelled Beltane. This Celtic holiday, called a Sabbat (which loosely means "day of rest"), is observed on May 1, celebrating the sacred marriage of the Goddess and the God and the fruit of their union which is all living things.

BCE or B.C.E.—A time designation meaning "before the common era," which is synonymous with B.C.

Black magick—A name applied to any negative magickal working. People who regularly indulge in this practice are sometimes said to be on the "left handed path."

Blockader—The mountain term for a person who makes and sells illegal whiskey.

Book of Shadows—A magickal diary kept by a religious Witch. Some say the unusual name came from years of having to hide the workings from church authorities, and others say it means that an unworked spell or ritual is a mere shadow, not taking form until enacted.

Calvinism—A Christian fundamentalist religious doctrine, named for founder John Calvin (1509-1564), which teaches pre-destination, literal interpretation of the Bible, and God's favoritism toward certain individuals and institutions. This thinking flourished in Great Britain's Protestant reform movement, and has had a great impact on the religious character of Appalachia.

Cauldron—A deep iron pot which was a common magickal tool in the Celtic Pagan traditions. It was a practical object as well, one which could be used for cooking or washing in addition to making magick. In Celtic mythology, the cauldron is symbolic of the womb of the Mother Goddess in which all life begins, ends, and regenerates.

CE or C.E.—A time designation meaning "common era," synonymous with A.D.

Celtic—Pertaining to the Celts, a war-like tribe of early Europe who eventually settled in northern France, Britain, and Ireland between 800 and 500 B.C.E. Celtic magickal practices and beliefs heavily influence Appalachian folk magick.

Charivari—An old American ritual which probably boasts Pagan roots. This involves making lots of celebratory noise at the consummation of a marriage, with the newlywed groom forcibly taken from his bride's bed and harassed. Also spelled chivaree and shivaree. Possibly related to the Middle English term "chivalrous."

Charm—1) An item or talisman which is magickally charged to a specific intent, or 2) a simple chant usually consisting of one or two couplets, which helps seal a spell. The second definition is the most common one in Appalachia but, because theirs is a largely oral tradition, virtually all of the original old charms have been lost to us over the past fifty years as the practice of folk magick fell from favor.

Appendix C: Glossary of Terms

Clan—A Gaelic word referring to an extended family.

Conscious mind—That part of the brain to which we have access in the course of a normal, waking day. It is the part of the mind which holds retrievable memory and other easy-to-recall information.

Coven—From the same root word as "convene," meaning to come together. A coven is a group of two or more Witches (or witches) who regularly meet to work magick, worship together, and provide the companionship of like minds. Despite the negative connotations the word has developed over the past several centuries, coven gatherings are no more sinister than Sunday church meetings.

Curse—A pronouncement of evil laid upon a person, place, or object by another person. In Appalachia, curses are believed to be placed by witches or spirits.

Discarnate—A non-corporeal being. A human discarnate is also called a ghost or, in Appalachia, a haint.

Divination—A method of looking into the future or unknown past, or for seeking out hidden answers to questions.

Dowser—See water witch.

Faery—Also spelled fairy and faerie. A nature spirit.

Familiar—An animal who is the working partner and/or servant of a witch.

Fetch—A spectral, human duplicate which is believed to appear to someone who will die within a fortnight. Sometimes referred to as a doppelgänger, the fetch has its origins in Scotland.

Feud—From the Anglo-Saxon *foehth* meaning "hostile." A violent disagreement of long standing between two mountain clans.

Folk magick—The magick of the common people which has been passed down for generations.

Folk medicine—The cures of the common people which usually fall outside the prescribed practice of mainstream medical professionals. Folk medicine is sometimes called "natural medicine."

Folklore—The body of common knowledge of a culture, including its myths and legends, daily and holiday customs, beliefs in the paranormal, and its folk magick and rituals.

Folkways—The actual practice of living one's folklore.

Foxfire—1) The mysterious lights which float just above the ground in the distance but which, when approached, move away. 2) A luminescent substance of unknown origin which clings to the base of trees and logs in Appalachia.

Funeral trail—A prescribed path for a funeral procession to follow to the burial ground.

Gorm—A mountain colloquialism for the human soul or life force. The precise origin of the term is unknown.

Granny woman—A midwife, healer, and witch.

Graveyard magick—Any spell or rite performed in, or which uses an item taken from, a cemetery as a catalyst for magickal success. The mechanics, and the perceived safety, of this practice varies between magickal traditions.

Haint—Mountain vernacular for ghost or spirit.

Herbalism—The knowledge of and use of herbs and plants for either magickal or medicinal purposes.

Hypnagogic sleep—The light sleep state entered into just before falling asleep or just before awakening. At this point the mind is in the perfect state of receptivity for divination.

Incense—The smoking of herbs, oils, or other aromatic items which can both scent the air and impart magickal energies to an area.

Kinfolk—Derived from the Middle English kyn, it means a relative. Also used are the gender specific "kinsman" and "kinswoman."

Liver-grown—A belief found both in Appalachia and the Ozarks that an infant's liver can grow to the side of its body, causing lifelong illnesses and crippling. Tests and cures are often painful, if not outright abusive, and are usually performed by witches and granny women.

Lych—An Old English word for "corpse" which is still used in Appalachia.

Magick—Spelled in this text with a 'k' to differentiate it from the magic of stage illusion. Probably the best definition of magick was coined by infamous ceremonial magician Aleister Crowley almost a century ago: "Magick is the science and art of causing change to occur in conformity to will."

Magickal circle—A sacred space set aside for magickal working or as a protected area.

Magickal community/people—1) The collective body of people who attempt to live a magickal lifestyle either through their cultural patterns or their religious beliefs. 2) All people who practice any form of magick.

Magickal diary—A record of needs, spells, successes and failures, and all things which may have influenced the outcome, such as weather, moon phases, etc.

Magickal substitution—The act of offering a sacrifice in order to obtain a magickal goal. Example: killing and burying an animal as part of a spell to save a human life.

Moonshine—Slang term for home-brewed whiskey.

Native American—Pertaining to the indigenous people of North America (ie; American Indians) who predate the European exploration.

Nunnehi—Nature spirits of the Great Smokey Mountains who were friendly with the Cherokee.

Pagan—Derived from the Latin *paganus* meaning "of the earth." The follower of any one of the old nature/earth religions of the world.

Pendulum—Any heavy object suspended by a thread, chain, or string which can be held stationery at one end while the other is allowed to move to indicate answers to questions asked.

Poppet—An obsolete term for a doll, particularly when referring to one which is used to represent a specific person in a magickal spell where a binding effect is desired. Poppets have long been associated with the negative aspects of manipulative magick, but they also serve positive purposes.

Portent—See omen.

Occult—The word occult literally means "hidden" and is broadly applied to a wide range of metaphysical topics which lie outside of the accepted realm of mainstream theologies. Such topics include, but are not limited to, divination, hauntings, spirit communication, natural magick, ceremonial magick, alternative spirituality, psychic phenomena, alchemy, astrology, demonology, and the study of the spiritual practices of ancient civilizations.

Omen—Any object, configuration, sight, sound, etc., which when seen or heard is believed to foretell future events.

Samhain—The Celtic holiday, called a Sabbat, which was celebrated on what is now Halloween, October 31. Samhain marked the beginning of winter for the Celts and was also their New Year's Day. Samhain is a time when the dead are honored. It also marks the official end of the harvest season.

Scrying—The act of gazing gently into water, fire, glass, or other reflective surface while concentrating on an issue or question. With practice, images and/or symbols will appear as an answer.

Second sight—To be able to see into the future or the spirit world, see events happening at a remote location, and/or accurately read omens. The term is synonymous with "clairvoyance."

Spell—A specific magickal ritual designed for the purpose of obtaining, banishing, or changing one particular condition.

Still—A homemade device for brewing whiskey. The word itself is a diminutive form of the verb "distill," meaning to extract by trickling down or to rectify.

Sympathetic magick—The belief that like attracts like. For example, if you need to get money you would work a spell which asks that you place some money in your pocket in order to attract more.

Talisman—A manmade object, often containing natural materials, which is used for personal protection or as a charm against evil influences.

Tall tale—A legend so exaggerated that no one truly believes it.

Water witch—A witch who has the ability to locate hidden, underground water sources.

White mule—Another mountain term for home-brewed whiskey.

Witch—1) In Appalachia, a witch is someone who can heal, lay on or remove curses, follows no particular faith, and who may be known or unknown to the community. 2) A follower of any of the old Pagan religions of western Europe. In this text a distinction between these two definitions is made by capitalizing the "w" when referring to adherents of the religion(s).

Wort—An obsolete term for "weed" or "herb."

Bibliography and Source Materials

(Partially Annotated)

Baker, Margaret. *Folklore and Customs of Rural England*. Totowa, NJ: Rowman and Littlefield, Co., 1974.

Baring-Gould, Sabine. *Curious Myths of the Middle Ages*. New York: Longman, 1897.

Baum, Joseph. *The Beginner's Handbook of Dowsing*. New York: Crown Publishers, Inc., 1974.

Bolyard, Judith A. *Medicinal Plants and Home Remedies of Southern Appalachia*. Springfield, IL: Thomas Press, 1965.

Brooks, Maurice. *The Appalachians* (Vols. I and II). Boston: Houghton Mifflin Co., 1965.

Brown, Raymond Lamont. *A Book of Superstitions*. New York: Taplinger Publishing Co., 1970.

Brunvand, Jan H. *The Study of American Folklore: An Introduction* (3rd edition). New York: W. W. Norton, Co., 1986. Good text for teaching how to read folklore with an eye to rooting out the underlying messages and practices they conceal.

Buckland, Raymond. *Scottish Witchcraft*. St. Paul, MN: Llewellyn Publications, 1991.

Campbell, John C. *The Southern Highlander and His Homeland*. New York: Russell Sage, Co., 1921.

Caranan, Guy and Candie, eds. *Voices From the Mountains*. New York: Alfred A. Knopf, 1975. Primary source material on economic conditions and on preservation of the old ways.

Carden, Gary. *Belled Buzzards, Hucksters and Grieving Specters*. Asheboro, NC: Down Home Press, 1994.

Castleman, Michael. *The Healing Herbs*. Emmaus, PA: Rodale Press, 1991.

Caudill, Harry M. *Night Comes to the Cumberlands: A Biography of a Depressed Area*. Boston: Little, Brown and Co., 1962. A look at the economic history of the region and the impact of attempts at financial assistance.

_____. *The Watchers of the Night*. Boston: Little, Brown and Co., 1976. A sequel to *Night Comes to the Cumberlands*.

Caudill, Rebecca. *My Appalachia: A Reminiscence*. New York: Hart, Rineholt and Winston, 1966.

Chaundler, Christine. *The Book of Superstition*. Secaucus, NJ: Citadel Press, 1970.

Cunningham, Scott. *Cunningham's Encyclopedia of Magical Herbs*. St. Paul, MN: Llewellyn Worldwide, 1986. An indispensable guide to the magickal properties of herbs.

Dabney, Joseph Earl. *Mountain Spirits*. New York: Charles Scribner's Sons, 1974.

Dargan, Olive T. *Highland Annals*. New York: Scribner and Sons, 1925.

Daugneaux, Christine B. *Appalachia: A Separate Place A Unique People*. Parsons, West Virginia. McClain Printing Company. 1981.

Dorson, Richard M. *Folklore and Folklife: An Introduction*. Chicago: The University of Chicago Press, 1972.

Draper, L. C. *King's Mountain and Its Heroes*. Cincinnati, OH: Thomason Press, 1881.

Emrich, Duncan. *Folklore on the American Land*. Boston: Little, Brown and Co., 1972.

Fielding, William J. *Strange Superstitions and Magical Practices*. New York: The Paperback Library, 1966.

Ford, Henry J. *The Scotch-Irish in America*. Princeton, NJ: Princeton University Press, 1915. Contains a chapter tracing the route the Highland clans took when they fled Scotland after their defeat by the English at Culloden and how this flight affected the worldview of the Appalachian people.

Gainer, Patrick W. *Witches, Ghosts and Signs: Folklore of the Southern Appalachians*. Grantsville, WV: Seneca Books, 1975.

Gazaway, Rena. *The Longest Mile*. Garden City, NY: Doubleday and Co., Inc., 1969.

Hand, Wayland D., ed. *The Frank C. Brown Collection of North Carolina Folklore*, Vols. 1–7. Durham, NC: Duke University Press, 1964. Superb collection of Appalachian folkways nicely categorized into fourteen divisions, one of which includes native witchcraft and magickal practices. The earlier two-volume set (published in 1957) might be found at a local university library.

Hanley, Clifford. *The Scots*. New York: New York Times Books, 1980.

Harrison, Michael. *The Roots of Witchcraft*. Secaucus, NJ: The Citadel Press, 1974. Gives information on the view of witches in the late medieval period, one which heavily influences the ancestors of the mountaineers.

Hoffman, Edwin D. *Fighting Mountaineers: The Struggle For Justice in Appalachia*. Boston: Houghton Mifflin Co., 1979. A look at the legal concerns of mountain people, many of which involve religious freedom issues.

Hutchens, Alma R. *Indian Herbalogy of North America*. Windsor, ON: Merco (fifteenth edition), 1989.

Jones, Loyal, and Billy Edd Wheeler. *Laughter in Appalachia: A Festival of Southern Humor*. Little Rock, AR: August House, 1986.

Jones, Virgil Carrington. *The Hatfields and the McCoys*. Chapel Hill: The University of North Carolina Press (sixth printing), 1979. A study of what is probably the most famous clan feud in modern history. In the fifty-plus years that the battle raged, at least sixty-five people were killed.

Kephart, Horace. *Our Southern Highlanders*. Knoxville, TN: The University of Tennessee Press, 1976.

Lehner, Ernst. *Folklore and Symbolism of Flowers, Plants and Trees*. New York: Tudor Publishing Co., 1960. An excellent primer for learning the beliefs upon which much of European and North American folk magick is based.

Marshall, Catherine. *Christy*. New York: Avon Books, 1967. Though this is a work of fiction, it is based on the experiences of the author's mother who went to teach in the mountains in 1912. It is probably one of the most realistic, and most entertaining, looks at Appalachian life in this century which exists.

Mathes, C. Hodge. *Tall Tales From Old Smokey*. Kingsport, TN: Southern Publishers, Inc., 1952. Tales of the traditional storyteller collected.

McCoy, Edain. *Celtic Myth and Magick*. St. Paul, MN: Llewellyn Worldwide, 1995. Looks at a wide range of Celtic magickal beliefs and practices.

_____. *A Witch's Guide to Faery Folk*. St. Paul, MN: Llewellyn Worldwide, 1994.

McLynn, Frank. *The Jacobites*. New York: Routledge and Kegan Paul, Inc., 1985. Looks at the heart of the conflict between the English and the followers of Bonnie Prince Charlie who immigrated to Appalachia in the mid-eighteenth century.

Mercatante, Anthony S. *The Magic Garden: The Myth and Folklore of Flowers, Plants, Trees and Herbs*. San Francisco: Harper and Row, 1976.

Muir, Frank. *Christmas Customs and Traditions*. New York: Taplinger Publishing Co., 1975.

Page, Linda Garland, and Hilton Smith, eds. *The Foxfire Book of Appalachian Toys and Games* (second edition). Chapel Hill: The University of North Carolina Press, 1993.

Peattie, Roderick, ed. *The Great Smokies and the Blue Ridge*. New York: Vanguard Press, 1943. Though written as a history and travelogue, this book contains wonderful insights into the character of the mountain people.

Pei, Mario. *The Story of English*. Philadelphia: Lippincott, 1952.

Porter, Elliot. *Appalachian Wilderness: The Great Smoky Mountains*. New York: Ballantine Books, 1973.

Reader's Digest Association, Inc., The. *American Folklore and Legend*. Pleasantville, NY: Reader's Digest General Books, 1978.

Reynolds, George P. and students, eds. *Foxfire 9*. New York: Doubleday and Co., 1986.

Richardson, Ethel Park, and Sigmund Spaeth, eds. *American Mountain Songs*. New York: Greenburg, 1955 (originally published in 1927).

Roberts, Bruce. *Where Time Stood Still*. New York: Crowell-Collier Press, 1970.

Ross, Anne. *Everyday Life of the Pagan Celts*. New York: G. P. Putman's Sons, 1970.

Russell, Randy. *Mountain Ghost Stories and Curious Tales*. Winston-Salem, NC: J.F. Blair, 1988.

Shackelford, Laurel and Bill Weinberg, eds. *Our Appalachia: An Oral History*. New York: Hill and Wang, 1977.

Sharp, Cecil, and Olive D. Campbell. *English Folk Songs in the Southern Appalachians*, Vols. I and II. London: Oxford University Press, 1932.

Shelton, Ferne. *Pioneer Comforts and Kitchen Remedies: Old Timey Highland Secrets From the Blue Ridge and Great Smoky Mountains*. High Point, NC: Hutcraft, 1965.

Shepherd, Muriel E. *Cabins in the Laurel*. Chapel Hill: The University of North Carolina Press, 1935. Interesting guide to the mindset of the mountaineer, including some folk magickal beliefs.

Thomas, Jean. *Ballad Making in the Mountains of Kentucky*. New York: Oak Publications, 1964 (originally published in 1939). Excellent musicological study. Examines the links to Anglo-Celtic music and delves into modern ballads as a form of storytelling and myth keeping.

Tuleja, Tad. *Curious Customs*. New York: Harmony Books, 1987.

Walker, Barbara G. *The Crone: Woman of Age, Wisdom, and Power*. San Francisco: HarperCollins, 1985.

Walsh, William S. *Curiosities of Popular Custom*. Philadelphia: J. B. Lippincott, Co., 1898.

Wigginton, Eliot, ed. *The Foxfire Book*. Garden City, NY: Doubleday and Co., 1972. The first Foxfire book began as an experimental magazine created by a high school English class in Appalachian Georgia. The students began collecting information about the old ways from the elderly persons in their community. The books have been wildly popular and are highly recommended to anyone wanting to learn more about the Appalachians and the folk magick to be found there.

_____. *Foxfire 2*. Garden City, NY: Doubleday and Co., 1973.

_____. *Foxfire 4*. Garden City, NY: Doubleday and Co., 1977.

_____. *Foxfire 5*. Garden City, NY: Doubleday and Co., 1979.

_____. *Foxfire 7*. Garden City, NY: Doubleday and Co., 1981. This volume is almost exclusively dedicated to examining various aspects of Appalachian religion—including some beliefs about the origin of paranormal occurrences.

Wigginton, Eliot and Margie Bennett, eds. *Foxfire 10*. New York: Doubleday, 1993.

Wilson, Charles Morrow. *Backwoods America*. Chapel Hill, NC: The University of North Carolina Press, 1934.

Other Source Material on Appalachian Folkways

Also useful to any study of Appalachian folk magick are the journals of the folklore societies of Appalachian states and folklore institutes, some of which are now out of print. Numerous articles in the back issues of the journals of folklore societies of West Virginia and Kentucky were especially helpful in gleaning insights into mountain beliefs. North Carolina and Tennessee have also published similar magazines. Check with university libraries in your area for the availability of back copies.

Additional Source Material on General Folk Magick

Though not used to compile this text, the following titles all give specific spells or provide more information on the mechanics of folk magick. They are available through the publisher of this book, unless otherwise noted. Please see the "Stay in Touch" section following the index for more information.

By Aima: *The Ritual Book of Herbal Spells* (Foibles).

By Raymond Buckland: *Secrets of Gypsy Dream Reading*; *Gypsy Love Magick*; *Secrets of Gypsy Fortunetelling*.

By Scott Cunningham: *The Complete Book of Incense, Oils and Brews*; *Crystal, Gem and Metal Magic*; *Magical Herbalism*; *Earth Power*; *Earth, Air, Fire and Water*; *The Magic in Food*.

By Scott Cunningham and David Harrington: *The Magical Household*; *Spell Crafts*.

By Mary Devine: *Magic From Mexico*.

By Ray T. Malbrough: *Charms, Spells and Formulas*.

By Trish Telesco: *The Kitchen Witch's Cookbook*; *A Witch's Brew*; *A Victorian Grimoire*.

By Doreen Valiente: *Natural Magic* (Phoenix).

Llewellyn Annuals: *The Organic Gardening Almanac*, *The Magical Alamanac*, *The Moon Sign Book*.

Index

– A –

acupressure, 158, 191

acupuncture, 58, 191

Alzheimer's Disease, 47

ancestor/s, 3–4, 23, 36, 61, 89, 92, 102, 119, 121, 150–151, 175–176, 178, 201

arthritis/rheumatism, 47–48

Arthur, King, 21, 146

Ash Wednesday, 67

asthma, 48

astrology, 115, 191, 196

ax, 149

– B –

backaches, 49, 157

banshee, 29

battle, 6, 20, 201

Bealtaine (May 1), 67, 103, 116, 130, 191

bean/s, 30, 47, 66, 96, 98, 106, 116, 187, 190

"bedding the bride", 138

bees, 48, 121–122, 155

bell, 20, 80

Bigfoot, 35

bird/s, 25–26, 43, 49, 76–77, 122, 127, 130, 179

black, 21, 28, 42–43, 46, 49, 51, 53–54, 60, 62–63, 67, 77, 85, 93, 113, 121, 152, 191

black lung, 49

bladder infections, 50

blockader/s, 192

blood, 6, 26, 38, 47, 51, 54, 59, 61, 63, 65–66, 105, 150, 156

Blue Ridge Mountains, 5

Bonnie Prince Charlie, 6, 202

bread, 48, 51, 102–103, 105, 113, 116, 134–135, 176, 179, 187

Britain, 9, 20–21, 25, 80, 96, 143, 153, 192

broom/s, 37, 92, 95, 118, 126

burns, 50, 143, 156–157

– C –

cancer, 49, 62, 64–65, 115, 120

candle/s, 33, 51, 58, 86, 92, 107, 143, 171

cat, 31

caul, 158–159

cauldron, 87, 93, 192

caves, 118

Celts/Celtic, 4, 9, 11, 13, 17, 21–22, 25, 29, 32, 38–39, 63, 67, 76, 78, 82, 86, 90–93, 96, 117, 121, 128, 130–131, 155, 157, 160, 174–175, 191–192, 196, 202

ceremonial magick, 2, 17, 196

charcoal, 153–154, 182

charms/chants, 32–34, 55–56, 87, 94–95, 99, 107, 109–111, 130, 132, 134–135, 149, 167, 192, 196, 204

Cherokee, 4, 36, 50, 91, 185, 195

chicken/s, 62–63, 76, 147, 158, 187–189

child/children, 3, 11, 20–21, 51, 98, 119, 122, 135, 147–149, 151–153, 155–165, 167–169, 172–173

childbirth, 80, 147, 149, 151, 153, 155, 157, 159, 161, 163, 165, 167

chimney, 53–54, 77, 92–93, 95, 107

Christmas, 11, 163, 202

Christy, 201

clan/s, 1, 4, 6, 11, 13, 21–23, 101, 103, 137, 193, 200–201

clock, 20, 28, 31, 68, 160, 165–166

clothing/clothes, 3, 49, 67, 112, 148, 152, 160, 162

cloven-hooved animals, 88, 90

coal, 49, 161

colds/flu, 51–52

color, 27, 67, 69, 71, 112–113, 121

company, 98–99, 124, 182

contraception, 52

cooking, 92, 108, 110, 113–114, 171, 187–189, 192

corn, 52, 65, 116, 131–132, 136, 149, 152, 184, 187

corpse (see lych), 19–20, 194

cow/s, 8, 43, 47, 50–51, 64, 76, 86, 122–123, 132, 134

cramps, 52–53

creation myth, 122

crying, 31, 77, 160

Cumberland Mountains, 5

curse/s, 3, 8, 10, 25–27, 37–38, 93, 95–97, 102–103, 105–107, 109–110, 112, 126–127, 162, 193, 197

Index

cuts/lacerations, 26, 34, 38, 48, 53–55, 62, 67, 96, 102–103, 110, 118, 121, 132–133, 140, 157, 162, 167, 179, 184, 188–189

– D –

death, 19–23, 25–31, 33, 35–37, 39, 46, 62, 80, 93, 98, 109, 117, 121, 157, 159

Devil/Satan, 7–9, 26, 31, 42–43, 52, 64, 88, 107, 123

diarrhea, 53–54

dog/s, 26–27, 29, 31, 54, 57, 76, 98, 121, 132, 134, 136

doll/s, 131, 145, 149, 195

door/s, 31, 33, 38, 74, 85, 95–100, 107, 111, 122, 127, 138, 162

dowsers (see water witches), 11–12, 193

dream/s, 28, 47, 60, 68, 104–106, 110, 113–114, 128, 130, 132, 153, 161, 176, 182, 191, 204

Dublin, 6

– E –

earaches, 54

Easter, 103, 108

edema, 54

egg tree, 108

enemy/ies, 36–37, 52, 106

England/English, 6–7, 11, 17, 19–20, 39, 80, 91, 105, 110, 132, 134, 137, 192, 194, 199–200, 202–203

epidemics, 29, 46, 75

ethics, 15–16, 143, 174

expectorants, 42, 52

– F –

faery meadows, 35–36

feathers, 158

fertility, 52, 60, 80, 84, 96, 107–108, 113–114, 124, 135–136, 138, 147–151, 153, 155, 157, 159, 161, 163, 165, 167

feud/s, 6, 99, 101, 105, 137, 193, 201

fever, 42, 46, 55–56

fidelity, 113–114, 125, 127, 129, 131, 133, 135–137, 139, 141–143

fire, 37, 54, 56, 77, 80, 85–86, 89–90, 93, 105–106, 115, 149, 196, 204

fireplace (also see hearth), 32, 51, 92–96, 107, 130, 143, 156, 184

fishing, 120

fits/epilepsy, 55, 62, 158

folk medicine, 41–42, 44, 193

folklore, 1, 7, 17, 26, 30, 32, 39, 71, 75, 92, 107, 110, 124, 126, 184, 193–194, 199–202, 204

foxfire, 18, 28, 39–40, 71, 124, 170, 172, 194, 202–203

fractures, 56

fundamentalist, 9, 21, 41, 192

funeral trails, 20–21, 23–24, 38, 122, 128, 194

– G –

Georgia, 4–5, 35, 78, 203

ghost/s (also see haint/s), 9, 12, 20, 24, 27, 30–34, 39, 104, 119, 168, 171, 193–194

Good Friday, 116

gout, 57

granny woman/women, 10–11, 41, 57–58, 68, 75, 78, 126, 148, 158–159, 163, 194

graveyard, 2, 4, 6, 8, 10, 12, 14, 16, 18–20, 22–24, 26, 28, 30, 32–34, 36, 38, 40, 42–44, 46, 48–50, 52–54, 56–58, 60, 62, 64, 66, 68, 70, 74, 76, 78, 80, 82, 84, 86, 88, 90, 92, 94, 96, 98, 100, 102, 104, 106, 108–110, 112, 114, 116, 118–120, 122, 124, 126–128, 130, 132–134, 136, 138, 140, 142, 144–146, 148, 150, 152, 154, 156, 158, 160, 162, 164, 166–168, 170, 172, 174–180, 182, 184, 186, 188, 190, 192, 194, 196, 198, 200, 202, 204, 206, 208, 210, 212

Great Smoky Mountains, The, 5, 185, 202

Groundhog Day, 76

– H –

hail, 76, 85, 87–88

haint/s (also see ghost/s), 12, 19, 21, 23, 25, 27, 29–35, 37, 39, 170, 193–194

hair, 25, 37, 48, 55, 57–58, 65–66, 79, 110, 119, 126, 128, 140, 144–145, 156, 162, 167, 176

Halloween, 38, 196

harvest, 20, 77, 102, 116, 196

head, 3, 25, 27, 33, 43, 49, 54–55, 58, 60, 73, 81–84, 106, 115–116, 118, 131–132, 137, 143, 152, 160, 164, 168

headaches, 58

hearth (also see fireplace), 34, 37, 86, 91–95, 97, 99, 101, 103, 105, 107, 109, 111, 113, 115, 117, 119, 121, 123, 135, 149, 156

hen/s, 4, 17, 26, 31, 51, 95, 200

hepatitis, 59

horse/s, 28, 32, 42–43, 48–49, 58, 66, 76, 96, 151

horseradish, 32, 43, 48, 58

Houston, Sam, 4

hunting, 120–121, 124

– I –

insomnia, 60

Ireland/Irish, 6–7, 13, 20, 22, 25, 37, 95–96, 117, 124, 155, 157, 192

iron, 36, 46, 93, 96, 112, 192

– J –

jackro, 37

– K –

Kerault, Charles, 200, 203

kiss/ing, 22, 61, 128, 132

knife, 34, 87, 127, 153, 158, 179, 189

knitting, 110, 112, 157

– L –

Lammas (August 1), 116

laying on of hands, 67

lightning, 32, 74, 77, 85–86, 89

liver-grown, 194

Loch Ness Monster, 35

lodestones, 101

London, 6, 17, 39, 203

longevity, 19, 159

lych, 19, 22–24, 42, 170, 194

– M –

magickal substitution, 26, 65, 85–86, 195

malaria, 61

mattress, 49, 52, 60, 142, 144, 153, 158

menstruation, 147

mirror, 33, 96, 104–105, 128, 130, 151

miscarriage, 153, 155–156, 168

money, 3, 11, 164, 196

moon, 9, 14, 24, 52, 63–64, 78, 101, 107, 115–116, 118, 120–121, 124, 135, 145, 150, 153, 155–156, 163, 195, 204

moonshine, 48, 53, 63, 67, 71, 106, 195

murder, 22

music, 111, 165, 181, 183, 203

myrtle, 43, 61, 114, 130, 132, 134, 136

– N –

nail clippings, 55–56, 101–102, 176

nettles, 49–50, 65, 189

New Year's Day, 103, 196

nightmares, 32, 60, 105–106

North Carolina, 5, 17, 34, 201–204

nosebleed, 61

Nunnehi, 36, 195

– O –

occupation, 50, 165

omen/s, 3, 8, 24–26, 28–29, 39, 60, 76, 92–93, 97–98, 101–102, 118, 120, 122–123, 125–126, 130, 137, 142–143, 148, 156–157, 159–160, 195–196

owl/s, 26, 39, 77, 122

– P –

Pagan, 7–9, 11, 17, 21, 24, 31, 33, 38, 56, 67, 76, 80, 82, 84, 89–90, 93–94, 103, 107, 116–117, 119, 122, 124, 126, 128, 138, 145, 154–155, 163–164, 192, 195, 197, 202

pain, 47–48, 50, 54, 57, 65, 74, 158–159, 191

pendulum/s, 16, 140–142, 146, 195

poppets, 131–133, 145, 195

poverty, 6, 119, 156, 160

praying rocks, 170

pregnancy, 52, 147, 151–152, 157

protection, 19, 23, 25, 36–37, 39, 80, 85–87, 92, 95–96, 102, 107–108, 114, 136, 154–155, 160, 196

– Q –

quarrel, 93, 101–102

quilt/s, 127–129, 162

– R –

rain, 76, 79, 83–84, 88–89, 164

ravens, 25–26

Roosevelt, Franklin, 182

rooster, 26

rosemary, 43, 57, 93–94, 96, 114, 132, 135–136, 144, 188

rue, 32, 43, 94, 107, 114, 134–136, 158, 160

– S –

salt, 23–24, 54, 94–95, 101–102, 135, 187–190

salt water, 94, 101–102

Samhain (October 31), 38, 196

Sarasponda, 111

Satan (see Devil/Satan), 8, 26

Scotland/Scots/Scottish, 4, 6–7, 9, 13, 17, 23, 27, 29, 35, 37, 71, 90, 92, 110, 124, 146, 193, 199–201, 204

scrying, 104, 130, 196

shingles, 62–63

shivaree, 192

shoes, 3, 52, 97–98, 135, 137–139

Index

singing, 29, 58, 110–112, 164, 167

sleepwalking, 105

smoke, 54, 77, 93, 107, 158, 160

snake, 24, 42–43, 122, 124, 152

snakebite, 49, 85

sneeze/ing, 98, 158

snow, 51, 75, 77–79, 164

sourwood honey, 46, 48, 53, 63, 65, 67, 71

Spanish, 78

spider/s, 49, 51, 53–54, 61, 77, 122, 155

spider webs, 51, 53, 122

spinster/s, 110

spring equinox, 76

squash, 117–118

stomach, 51, 62–63, 65, 115, 120, 153, 156, 160, 162, 167

storytellers, 10, 13

sugar, 52, 65, 137, 161, 188–190

summer solstice, 76

superstition, 2–3, 200

– T –

taboo/s, 92, 102, 116–117, 126, 137, 148, 151–152, 157, 159

talisman/s, 36–37, 51, 135, 153–155, 162, 192, 196

Tallulah, Miss, 35

Tennessee, 5, 186, 204

The Beverly Hillbillies, 48, 126

The Waltons, 146

three, 10, 15, 27, 31–34, 37–38, 41, 49–50, 52, 54, 56, 58–59, 63–64, 66, 76–77, 81–82, 84, 93–94, 102, 105–106, 118, 132, 140, 148–149, 156, 158, 161–162, 167, 175, 189

threshold, 32, 96, 135

timber, 34

tonic, 46–47

toothache/s, 64

top, 52, 65, 76, 102, 109, 173, 189

tornado/es, 47, 75–76, 85, 87–89

Trail of Tears, The (1835), 4, 36

Triple Goddess, 39

tuberculosis, 42, 46, 49

– U –

umbilical cord, 157–158

urine, 44, 50, 54, 57, 60, 97, 105

– V –

violet/s, 19, 43, 58, 113, 128, 132–133, 136, 179

Virginia, 5, 46, 95, 129, 204

– W –

wake, 22

wand, 81, 84

warts, 65–66, 119

water witches, 10–11

weather, 9, 73–81, 83–85, 87, 89, 145, 164, 195

weaving, 110, 112

wedding, 63, 110, 126, 128–130, 135–140, 142, 149, 151, 156

wedding ring, 63, 129–130, 139–140, 142, 149, 151, 156

whip, 80–82, 188

whiskey (see moonshine), 22, 48–49, 65, 160, 190, 192, 195–196

wind, 31, 33, 73, 78, 80–83, 87, 89–90, 135, 160

window/s, 3, 26, 31–32, 58, 79, 87–88, 95–96, 102, 107, 110, 132–133, 138, 142, 162

winter, 11, 46, 51, 55, 75, 77–78, 103, 117, 163, 196

witch, 8–12, 15, 17, 37–39, 42–43, 66–68, 75, 81, 93, 104–105, 113, 118–119, 123–124, 146, 158, 163, 168, 170, 173, 192–194, 196–197, 202, 204

witch peg, 38

witchcraft, 8–10, 80, 90, 94, 105, 170, 179, 199, 201

wolf, 93, 127, 155

woodruff, 21, 43, 96, 106

– Y –

yeast infections, 66

Stay in Touch...

Llewellyn publishes hundreds of books on your favorite subjects

Order by Phone

Call toll-free within the U.S. and Canada, **1–800–THE MOON**.
In Minnesota call **(612) 291–1970**.
We accept Visa, MasterCard, and American Express.

Order by Mail

Send the full price of your order (MN residents add 7% sales tax) in U.S. funds to:

**Llewellyn Worldwide
P.O. Box 64383, Dept. K671-8
St. Paul, MN 55164-0383, U.S.A.**

Postage and Handling

(for the U.S., Canada, and Mexico)
- ◆ $4.00 for orders $15.00 and under
- ◆ $5.00 for orders over $15.00
- ◆ No charge for orders over $100.00

We ship UPS in the continental United States. We ship standard mail to P.O. boxes. Orders shipped to Alaska, Hawaii, The Virgin Island, and Puerto Rico are sent first-class mail.
Orders shipped to Canada and Mexico are sent surface mail.
International orders: Airmail—add freight equal to price of each book to the total price of order, plus $5.00 for each non-book item (audiotapes, etc.). Surface mail—Add $1.00 per item. Allow 4–6 weeks delivery on all orders. Postage and handling rates subject to change.

Group Discounts

We offer a 20% quantity discount to group leaders or agents. You must order a minimum of 5 copies of the same book to get our special quantity price.

Free Catalog

Get a free copy of our color catalog, *New Worlds of Mind and Spirit*. Subscribe for just $10.00 in the United States and Canada ($30.00 overseas, airmail). Many bookstores carry *New Worlds*—ask for it!

The Sabbats
A New Approach to Living the Old Ways
Edain McCoy

The Sabbats offers many fresh, exciting ways to deepen your connection to the turning of the Wheel of the Year. This tremendously practical guide to Pagan solar festivals does more than teach you about the "old ways"—you will learn workable ideas for combining old customs with new expressions of those beliefs that will be congruent with your lifestyle and tradition.

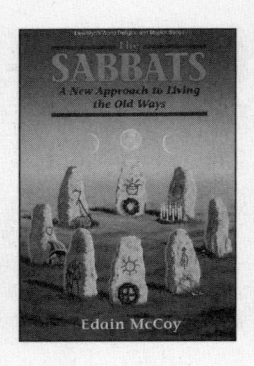

The Sabbats begins with background on Paganism (tenets, teachings, and tools) and origins of the eight Sabbats, followed by comprehensive chapters on each Sabbat. These pages are full of ideas for inexpensive seasonal parties in which Pagans and non-Pagans alike can participate, as well as numerous craft ideas and recipes to enrich your celebrations. The last section provides 16 complete texts of Sabbat rituals—for both covens and solitaries—with detailed guidelines for adapting rituals to specific traditions or individual tastes. Includes an extensive reference section with a resources guide, bibliography, musical scores for rituals, and more.

This book may contain the most practical advice ever for incorporating the old ways into your Pagan lifestyle!

1-56718-663-7, 7 x 10, 320 pp., illus., photos $14.95

To order, call 1-800-THE MOON
Prices subject to change without notice

Lady of the Night
A Handbook of Moon Magick & Ritual
Edain McCoy

Moon-centered ritual, a deeply woven thread in Pagan culture, is often confined to celebration of the full moon. Edain McCoy revitalizes the full potential of the lunar mysteries in this exclusive guide for Pagans who honor the Old Ways and seek new ways to celebrate the Lady who is always young.

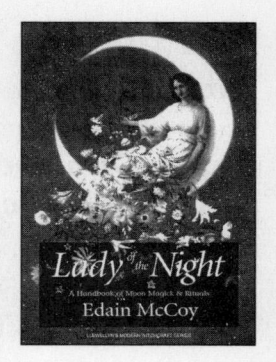

Lady of the Night explores the lore, rituals, and unique magickal potential associated with all phases of the moon: full, waxing, waning, moonrise/moonset and dark/new phases. Combined with an in-depth look at moon magick and suggestions for creating moon rituals that address personal needs, this is a complete system for successfully riding the tides of lunar magick.

Written for both solitary and group practice, this book is exceedingly practical and versatile. *Lady of the Night* reveals the masculine side of the moon through history and breaks new ground by showing how both men and women can Draw Down the Moon for enhanced spirituality. Pagans will also find fun and spirited suggestions on how to make the mystery of the moon accessible to non-Pagan friends and family through creative party planning and popular folklore.

1-56178-660-2, 240 pp., 7 x 10, illus., softcover $14.95

To order, call 1-800-THE MOON
Prices subject to change without notice

Ancient Ways
Reclaiming the Pagan Tradition
Pauline Campanelli
illus. by Dan Campanelli

Ancient Ways is filled with magick and ritual that you can perform every day to capture the spirit of the seasons. It focuses on the celebration of the Sabbats of the Old Religion by giving you practical things to do while anticipating the sabbat rites, and helping you harness the magical energy for weeks afterward. The wealth of seasonal rituals and charms are drawn from ancient sources but are easily performed with materials readily available.

Learn how to look into your previous lives at Yule . . . at Beltane, discover the places where you are most likely to see faeries . . . make special jewelry to wear for your Lammas Celebrations . . . for the special animals in your life, paint a charm of protection at Midsummer.

Most Pagans and Wiccans feel that the Sabbat rituals are all too brief and wish for the magick to linger on. *Ancient Ways* can help you reclaim your own traditions and heighten the feeling of magick.

0-87542-090-7, 256 pp., 7 x 10, illus., softcover $14.95

To order, call 1-800-THE MOON
Prices subject to change without notice

HexCraft
Dutch Country Pow-Wow Magick
Silver RavenWolf

The roots of American Witchcraft can be found in a 17th century settler tradition comprising Witchcraft and Native American magics. Now, the history and growth of this elusive tradition—called Pow-Wow—is analyzed in absorbing detail in *HexCraft*. *HexCraft* brings to life the chants, charms, spells and healing methods of a vital heritage that is nearly extinct today. Explore Hex Craft, also known as Pennsylvania Dutch Country Pow-Wow Magick—through the vivid examples and rare testimonials of those connected with its occult practices. Learn how to bring this Earth-honoring culture to life with the step-by-step instruction by Hex Craft-trained author Silver RavenWolf!

HexCraft presents Pow-Wow's simple nature and easy implementation in a format that encourages individual interpretation. More than a text book on magick or history, *HexCraft* will engage anyone interested in history, magick, spirituality or freedom of speech!

1-56718-723-4, 7 x 10, 320 pp., softcover $15.95

To order, call 1-800-THE MOON
Prices subject to change without notice

Jude's Herbal Home Remedies
Natural Health, Beauty & Home-Care Secrets
Jude C. Williams, M.H.

There's a pharmacy—in your spice cabinet! In the course of daily life we all encounter problems that can be easily remedied through the use of common herbs—headaches, dandruff, insomnia, colds, muscle aches, burns—and a host of other afflictions known to humankind. *Jude's Herbal Home Remedies* is a simple guide to self-care that will benefit beginning or experienced herbalists with its wealth of practical advice. Most of the herbs listed are easy to obtain.

Discover how cayenne pepper promotes hair growth, why cranberry juice is a good treatment for asthma attacks, how to make a potent juice to flush out fat, how to make your own deodorants and perfumes, what herbs will get fleas off your pet, how to keep cut flowers fresh longer … the remedies and hints go on and on!

Here are instructions for teas, salves, tinctures, tonics, poultices, along with addresses for obtaining the herbs. Dangerous and controversial herbs are also discussed. Grab this book and a cup of herbal tea, and discover from a Master Herbalist more than 800 ways to a simpler, more natural way of life.

0-87542-869-X, 240 pp., 6 x 9, illus., softcover $12.95

To order, call 1-800-THE MOON
Prices subject to change without notice